The Theatre Craft Book of Make-up, Masks, and Wigs

Edited and with
an introduction by

C. Ray Smith

THEATRE CRAFTS BOOKS
RODALE PRESS, INC.   EMMAUS, PA. 18049

Table of Contents

3

Introduction

by C. Ray Smith

"The Theatre Crafts Book of Makeup, Masks, and Wigs" could more simply have been called "The Theatre Crafts Book of Makeup," since makeup covers all three categories in the title. Each is a component activity of the craft of makeup whether it is used for disguise or for cosmetic purposes. Makeup is the generic name for the disguises that masks provide and of which wigs are a part. But in today's vernacular, the term connotes the more narrow field of painted makeup. This book aims at expanding that contemporary concept of the craft, so the fuller title is used to detail the specific categories within our scope.

In the past decade, if there has been a single direction in our art forms it has been the attempt to break down rigid categories—classifications that were built up by the idealists of preceding decades, categories that convince us all the more that life and individuality defy classification. In the past decade there has been

5

an attempt to accept all categories and activities and interests, if not quite equally, at least with less prejudice and exclusion than in the past. Iconoclasts have consistently stormed the barricades of habit and convention with the goal of eradicating them and permitting the intermingling of one side with the other, the interaction of each activity on the other. Painting became intermixed with sculpture so that we could not tell where one began and the other left off. Robert Rauschenberg and other painters added actual chairs and found objects as sculptural appendages to their painted canvases. In literature, fiction merged with non-fiction when Truman Capote wrote a non-fiction novel and Tom Wolfe and others expanded their reporting into the realm of playwrighting and poetry. In music, formal and popular works were interwoven by instrumentation, composition, and motifs. The Beatles and virtually every rock group that followed them, played updated Bach and other classical music, used gospel, hymn, and folk music to a flailing tribal beat. They orchestrated this vibrating, pulsating music for organ, violins, and classical sitar as well as for electric guitar. Silence, more and more, was included also as part of music since it was what occurs between musical sounds.

In the theatre, this musical device of John Cage became integral to Harold Pinter's plays, where the Pinterpause is nearly as significant as the Pinter word. Elsewhere in the theatre, this attempt to include more of our experience as part of the performance event coalesced as Environmental Theatre or The New Theatre. There, the distinctions between the stage and the auditorium, between the audience and the performer, between the performers' roles and the performers' personal lives, between the play and the discussion of it were continually erased and the elements intermeshed and intertwined.

In addition, all the arts during the past decade attempted systematic reversals of traditional subject matter and compositional conventions. The fine arts reached out to portray those areas that had been previously considered unacceptable or unworthy of designers' attention, to include the undesigned, the mediocre, the ordinary, even the boring. Artifacts from our popular culture—the kitchen, the automobile, the roadside, and industry—were the common materials used in uncommon ways, used out of context to produce what came to be known as pop art. These systematic reversals found any number of expressions in the theatre, but most patently pertinent to the subject of this book was the title of an Anthony Newley musical, which twisted the familiar nostalgic theatre slogan, "the smell of the grease paint," into the new vision of our perverse times, "The Roar of the Grease Paint, the Smell of the Crowd." Such are the fluctuating distinctions of our age of ambiguities.

Similarly, the distinctions between makeup, masks, and wigs are not rigid—perhaps never have been clear throughout the history of the craft. Makeup disguises have included 'character' face painting and war paint, masks of animals, spirits and grotesque beasts. Cosmetic makeup has included 'straight' face painting and other embellishments for the purposes of beautifying the performer. But traditional painted makeup ambiguously can create masks, as clowns and oriental traditions remind us.

Masks can become partial wigs or beards, as any picture book on the subject immediately reveals.

Understandably, therefore, the authors represented in this book discuss their subject across the broader board of makeup without regard to distinct categories of makeup activity. Though they may primarily discuss painted makeup, they may also take up the subject of wigs; though they primarily discuss wigs, they may also consider makeup or masks. Glenn Loney's article on television makeup includes a discussion with the show's hair designer; Patricia MacKay also considers both in her analysis of oriental makeup for a Peking Opera; Dick Smith, Joseph Cranzano, and Nicholas Kepros outline matters pertaining to hair and wigs as well as their primary subjects—painted and sculpted makeup. Richard Corson has written separate volumes on these subjects. Clearly, wigs are as much prosthetics as are the artificial elements of plastic face puffery that commonly go by that name; eyeglasses may be as well. The three aspects of makeup are usually inextricably intertwined.

8

Painted Makeup

In the world of fashion, painted makeup is thought to be as old as the Assyrian civilization, circa 2250 B.C., and was certainly used in ancient Egypt and in Rome. The Crusaders are said to have introduced it from the Middle East to Europe during the Middle Ages. But in the theatre, it appears to have been minimally used until the arrival of female actors, who brought their beautification techniques from the boudoir to the stage with great effect. Lady Wishfort in Congreve's "The Way of the World" describes the heaviness of the makeup in her 17th Century day, sighing sardonically, "Why, I am errantly flayed—I look like an old peeled wall."

Actual paint was apparently the first makeup —fraught with physical dangers because of its high lead content and its non-porosity. Everyone remembers the dangers that circus performers faced when they were swathed in gold paint for those glittering tableaux of "living statuary." As a consequence, using actual paints for makeup was ultimately rejected. Later, powders dominated makeup on and off stage, and crepe hair and spirit gum, cornstarch, burnt cork, and nose putty became the staples of the craft. Grease paints were first manufactured in the late 19th Century. Not quite a century has elapsed, in fact, since the first comprehensive manual in English devoted exclusively to makeup was published in 1877, and when the first grease paint sticks were announced. Tins and tubes of easy-to-apply grease paints followed; pancake and liquid makeup applied with sponges were a development of the 20th Century.

In the past several decades, newly developed plastics have changed the face of both street and theatrical makeups. Silicone, the most important new ingredient, produces a more durable natural look to makeups that once caked, crinkled, and gave performers an appearance of artificiality. Silicones make the new makeups even easier to apply and easier to remove. Other plastics are used in nose putty, for foam curlers and wig bases, and in new adhesives for prosthetic pieces. Plastics such as vinyl chloride ace-

9

tate in solution are built up in layers to make bald pates. As a sealing coat over makeup, polyvinyl alcohol is sometimes used. Plastic hair of acrylic and modacrylic fibers is also used for wig making. With these new materials, the time honored craft of makeup has developed its greater plasticity, in every sense, and its ever more accurate naturalism.

Naturalistic Makeup

In today's theatre and throughout "The Theatre Crafts Book of Makeup, Masks, and Wigs" three goals are constantly reaffirmed: They are the makeup technician's desire for continual variety of appearance, his concern for speed of application and speed of change if necessary, and his unquestioning choice of naturalness over artificiality.

In the modern theatre, although 'straight' cosmetic makeup and 'character' makeup are considered as equally important, both are approached predominantly in a naturalistic manner. The principal concerns of designers and craftsmen who work in this idiom are: different ages of characters; different weights—fat or slim faces; different races and national characteristics; various hair pieces—wigs, beards, moustaches, and sideburns; and special effects of blood, gore, and mutilation. Today's craft of makeup is primarily one of enhancement through concealment. It is a craft of painting on the face with all the techniques of naturalist painters in oil, tempera, or watercolor. Only in special cases does it include the craft of sculpting, when those prosthetic facial elements are used to build up character makeups. This tech-

nique might tend to merge with the art of mask making, since it is fragmented mask making, in effect. But it, too, is practiced almost exclusively in a naturalistic idiom; an idiom that virtually rejects the basic effects of masks.

Like the work of most makeup designers, current books on the subject concentrate on this craftsmanly prestidigitation of achieving nearly photographic portraiture as the single acceptable goal of makeup design. Naturalistic makeup dominates our conception of the craft in educational and community as well as in commercial theatre. This is a stylistic heritage of 19th Century naturalism, which has held the stage from Ibsen's day onwards, and which films and television have helped to protract into our age of abstraction and symbolism. In an age that has followed the great early 20th Century revolution in art—cubism, dada, the fauves—and which has expanded our vistas through abstract expressionism, pop, op, and funk art, the obsessive reliance on naturalism in theatre makeup seems vestigial.

One seemingly modern reversal has been a movement toward anti-makeup or non-makeup, which actors and critics have acclaimed as even greater than the admired feats of painted and sculpted faces. Extraordinary actors and actresses—from Henry Irving to Laurence Olivier, from Eleanora Duse to Helena Weigel—have achieved some of the most memorable makeups using only their bare faces as if they were masks. These non-makeups have been produced purely through muscular control of the face. Most makeup technicians, however, decry the effectiveness of this scale for makeup on the stage. There, they maintain, the distances from *acting area to audience make the facial expression too small for easy recognition. Yet the memory of a few brilliantly expressive faces on the stage is indelible.*

This approval of non-makeup influences the nigh-unto-battle controversy that rages between the different media. Several designers for film and television vie with each other in proving which medium makes the greater demands, which is the more detailed and refined makeup, which camera is the more perceptive, which of their crafts is the more meticulous and sensitive. The question is one of projection versus naturalism, of details, and of colors: All of the makeup technicians in the film media assault the coarseness and grossness that, they assert, makeup technicians in the theatre can get away with or must strive for. Yet many stage makeup people, including some of those who raise the controversy in this volume, have been trained in television, and many makeup artists who work in films were trained in makeup for the stage. Although this controversy makes for lively reading, he who elects to judge the victor may be worrying a back eddy.

The "no-makeup look," far from being the other side of the coin of a realistic approach is an extreme of naturalism. And naturalism, which attempts to recreate in as exact, literal, identical terms as possible the physical appearances of our existence, does not have the same view of the world as realism. Realism, most precisely, attempts to portray the spirit and the fact of our experience but also its totality. As a term, it should not be used interchangeably with naturalism, as is so common. Realism accepts the entirety of a situation in which, for example, an artificial convention appears, and the reality of its portrayal expresses the fact of that convention. What, then, is realism in makeup? Can any pure convention of our culture such as makeup ever be real? In fact, it can. Truly realistic makeup accepts the artificiality of the convention and finds a way to expose its overlay on nature in some honest, straightforward, direct and meaningful way.

The Makeup of Symbolism

Another approach to makeup has a more ancient heritage than naturalism yet may be even more attuned to the realistic tenor of our times. In current manuals of makeup technique, it is generally shunted off into the sidetrack of "special effects"—those supernatural reveries of beasts and monsters, ghouls, and gore. It is called "stylized" or "fantastic" makeup—terms that clearly imply a fundamentally pejorative judgment, terms that assume the superiority of the naturalistic idiom. Yet this other makeup idiom shares with the venerable tradition of masks a super-real or supra-real approach. It relies not on the recreation of physical actualities but on the creation of character symbols. This symbolic makeup proclaims the basic and primitive realities of the characters on the stage. It is a new realism that accepts the conventions of the art form—theatre—and reveals its abstract or non-realistic aspects in order to portray the total experience.

What this approach works with today is the new, more inclusive vision that permits all the artifacts of our visual environment to suggest,

13

to symbolize physical characteristics. Like pop art, the makeup of symbolism takes common materials and objects out of context, letting improvisation and make-do go hand in hand with make-believe. Designers who work in this vein recognize the artificiality of a wig, for example, and express its form with such "un-naturalistic" materials as cut paper, feathers, ruffled organdy, fur, net, wool yarn, rope, wood shavings, plastic strips, metal strips, wire, fabric strips, pipe cleaners, paper bags—any material at hand that they can fashion into the shape of a wig. This kind of designer recognizes the potential of painted makeup used frankly as masks, of colors and lines on the face blending in, merging with lines and colors of costumes. In this idiom, improvisation has the advantage of economy, yet the greatest benefits are the heights of imagination that designers scale. For in the makeup of symbolism, imagination is as crucial to a designer as his painterly craft.

It is a sign of our ambivalent time that paint is used to achieve naturalism while masks symbolize reality. In this makeup of symbolism and abstraction, as Irene Corey writes in "The Mask of Reality": "The designer is suddenly freed of dependence on the individual features of the actor, freed of the recognizable scale of the body. The whole world of invention is open, and he is limited only by the scope of his own observation and imagination. The only other restrictions come from the play itself, and from the goal set by the director." The invention and imagination of designers who work in this idiom rely on different sources of inspiration. In the makeup of naturalism, the sources are those examples that walk by us every day for our observation. In the makeup of symbolism, sources of inspiration are extended to art works that spring from the outer limits of artists' imaginations; they also include the inanimate objects of our daily existence. This view of makeup is discussed on the following pages in "Making Faces for Kids"—an article on makeup for children's theatre—although it has application throughout the non-naturalistic theatre and could add unexpected dimensions to the established naturalistic theatre.

Its related craft, masks, has been primarily makeup of symbolism and abstraction from the very beginning. Masks are symbolic in form and construction and they become symbols of sometimes enormous potency and authority in themselves. Ceremony and ritual, fetish and taboo, totem, superstition, and magic have been the messages of masks from primitive cultures down to our own, we assume, more sophisticated culture. What are today's messages transmitted by masks? Several articles in this volume approach the question. From the animal and spirit masks of ancient Egypt, of Aztec Mexico and Inca Peru, of China and Japan, Bali, Siam, Burma, Borneo, and Java, and of African tribes and North American and Alaskan Indians, these sculpted face coverings have demonstrated the deepest fantasies of the artist in man. Even Western Europe's death masks, dominoes, masked puppets, and Picasso's own African-inspired mask-like sculptures evoke these nebulous sensations of the unknown and the supernatural.

How can we fail to give masks their time honored dynamic authority in contemporary theatre? The few new and truly contemporary masks of painted fiberglas or vacuum formed

15

plastics do not constitute any measurable token of adequate interest. Seldom do we see productions, even of Greek plays, that attempt to recreate what we so certainly know of the power of masks. What this book may help to make forcefully clear is that the makeup of symbolism, the mainstream in which the history of masks has been carried along, is still a viable, vital, and potent force for our contemporary theatre, a force that more and more theatre people are attentively respecting.

The Literature on Makeup, Masks, and Wigs

On the subject of masks, the literature is enormous in the theatre category and in the art book categories. The literature on current techniques of naturalistic painted makeup is also extensive. Besides Richard Corson's "Stage Makeup" (Appleton-Century-Crofts, New York, 1967), which several of our authors specifically single out for praise, and Philippe Perrottet's "Practical Stage Makeup" (Reinhold Book Corporation, New York, 1967), Herman Buchman's "Stage Makeup' (Watson-Guptill Publications, New York, 1971), which was previewed in "Theatre Crafts" May/June 1971 issue but unfortunately not reprinted in this volume, are books that every student and professional of makeup should own. Richard Corson's "Fashions in Hair" (Peter Owen, London 1965, Revised 1971) has virtually become an order catalogue of 5000 hair styles and wig designs for most professionals and wig rental houses, and is certainly a required reference for all.

Almost no literature exists, however, on makeup and wigs for the non-naturalistic theatre of symbol and abstraction. With the exception of Irene Corey's "The Mask of Reality" (Anchorage Press, Kentucky, 1968), which so many other makeup books refer to without documenting and without credit to the makeup designer, there is no literature on this iconoclastic, sometimes pop approach to symbolic makeup. Other books give it token attention and a few isolated photographs. "The Theatre Crafts Book of Makeup, Masks, and Wigs" aims for a more balanced, expansive, and more inclusive view of makeup as a craft.

Most makeup books also offer lists of recommended makeup materials as well as an outlined program of studying the craft, and several of the authors in this book offer comparable outlines and materials lists. Most makeup teachers recommend collecting a file of photographs that might eventually make good models for makeup. We should note Richard Corson's recommendation in "Stage Make-up" of photographing one's completed makeup experiments as they are executed so as to show the comparative progress of a student in this ephemeral, evanescent craft.

17

With the possible exception of that equally ephemeral thing called acting, no craft of theatre is so clearly a craft as makeup, so clearly incapable of being taught, so clearly dependent on trial and error, on repetition and constant meticulous care. These basic crafts of theatre—acting and makeup—require the perfecting of techniques in person. Costume designers tell us how they go about designing for a costume house to realize their sketches. They, like set designers, are architects rather than builders. Makeup *designers, on the other hand, tell us how they personally execute their designs with a craftsmanship that they must develop in their own hands and eyes.*

Only in the past 20 years have makeup designers become indispensable members of a theatre producer's team. Before 1950, nearly all recognized and esteemed actors designed and executed their own makeups. Films and television helped to change that situation, along with the work of unions and the increasing specialization of our age. Some of the designers in this volume raise penetrating questions about their unions.

"The Theatre Crafts Book of Makeup, Masks, and Wigs" is an introduction to this specialized world of makeup. It ranges from philosophical questioning to how-to demonstrations. Several makeup designers trace their methodologies in step-by-step detail. This book does not pretend to be complete and comprehensive—how could it be? It does, however, present a student of makeup with the ideas, approaches, and techniques of more than a dozen distinguished teachers and experts in the field all collected into one volume. Richard Corson says of completeness on the subject that no one ever finishes learning to do makeup. "It is safe to say that you have not now learned to do makeup," he says at the conclusion of his manual, "you have only begun to learn."

18

ACKNOWLEDGMENTS

The editor is grateful to the designers, technicians, authors, photographers, and information offices who gave their advice, time, and energy so freely initially in the writing and presentation of individual articles for "Theatre Crafts" magazine. For their generosity in permitting those materials to be published in this volume for the benefit of students and lovers of the theatre, he is doubly grateful. The editor is also indebted to the staff of "Theatre Crafts" magazine, Patricia J. MacKay and Jody Brockway, for their care, concern, and perception in the preparation of this volume—especially for the clear and concise captions by Patricia MacKay on the step-by-step methodologies of applying makeup.

19

Contemporary makeup for the performing arts changes with the times, like everything else in our culture, but we seldom have any perspective on its meandering progress until a man of long experience muses for us about the old times. Somehow that kind of comparative view emphasizes and isolates the past for us, fixes and galvanizes our vision of the present.

Eddie Senz is a man of such long experience in theatrical makeup. He started in the business at the age of 14, apprenticing to his father at the Metropolitan Opera House during the era of Enrico Caruso. He worked with the Shuberts and Ziegfeld. He made Raymond Massey into Abe Lincoln. Grace Moore, Katherine Cornell, Alfred Lunt, Lynn Fontanne, Gertrude Lawrence, Laurette Taylor, Gloria Swanson, Valentino, Lily Pons, Robert Merrill, and Julie Andrews are just part of his star roster.

Over the years he has also worked with fashion photographers, for "Vogue" and "Harper's Bazaar," and has helped with the filmed images of politicians.

Since the Nixon-Kennedy television debates, makeup has come to play a large part in politicians' images. Yet long before those debates, Eddie Senz was making up public figures like Mayor LaGuardia, Wendell Wilkie, President Roosevelt, and Cardinal Spellman for newsreel and public appearances. He says, "Now men know that women voters not only evaluate a man be-

cause he is intellectually qualified, but also because he is visually attractive."

His father, Adolf Senz, was the makeup director of the Metropolitan Opera for 52 years. "He was a sharp taskmaster; I couldn't get away with anything," Eddie Senz recalls of his apprenticeship. In his own 40 year career he has pioneered makeup for virtually all the performing arts—opera, ballet, theatre (both musicals and drama), television and motion pictures (both black and white and color), and public appearances, speeches, and lectures.

Senz has been a makeup director for Paramount, Twentieth Century Fox, MGM, and Warner Brothers for over thirty years, and he was a pioneer in the development of color makeup for technicolor and cinerama as well as television.

From this long career Eddie Senz draws some tips and pointers, some reminiscences, and contemporary commentary in an interview that he hoped would be helpful to actors and students of drama. He also provides a historical perspective that professional makeup designers may use as a scale rule to measure the status of contemporary makeup. Besides, he warmly recalls some little known anecdotes on the not-too-far distant past of makeup.

The following interview was first published in "Theatre Crafts" in March/April, 1970.

21

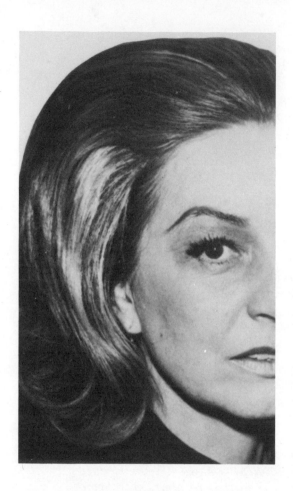

Makeup designer Eddie Senz has changed the face of many a star as well as of Peggy Senz, his wife, who modeled for a demonstration of before and after— without makeup (above) and madeup in character (right).

A Man of Many Faces

from an interview with Eddie Senz

Makeup is changing constantly. The direction of the changes is shaped by new ideas and new products. Makeups used to be quite heavy with a lot of pigment and substance that gave the skin the desired color but obliterated the texture. It looked dull and was very obvious. Today, we use a lot of makeups that go on quickly; we use a thinner foundation that doesn't cover the actor's natural color.

We used to use lights and shadows to create certain effects for character makeups—like hardening the labule fold line from the wing of the nose to the side of the mouth or elongating the nose. We used a lot of putties and waxes. Today, we actually make physical changes. A woman can make her eyes longer or wider by using a strip lash in the correct place. Instead of putties and waxes, we use prosthetic noses made out of light fluffy rubber. New lighting techniques, improved materials, the addition of latex and rubber have all added a three dimensional effect to make up.

Women's Makeup

In the past, especially on the stage, it has been obvious that the female lead had been made-up. The thing today is to create the illusion of natural beauty—of not having to use artificial aids. She should appear non-made-up.

The structural character is the first thing we think about. Color is significant, but only of secondary importance. For

23

example, if the lead must appear a pretty girl, and she has a very round face, small eyes or a badly shaped mouth, we can correct these things by changing her hair style, shaping the eyebrow, the mouth and choosing the right kind of neckline. We can make a round face look like the standard beautiful oval by piling hair on top of the head or cutting it in the correct way. But it cannot appear to be "beauty parlorish"

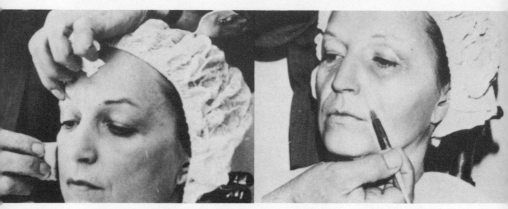

Eddie Senz demonstrates the steps in his "instant aging" makeup (pages 24–27): 1—foundation color is applied; 2—the face is modelled with highlights and shadows;

or "man-made." There is a tendency for female performers in contemporary plays to be effected by fashion trends, especially in eye makeup. The result often is a stylish actress, but one who is not as pretty as she could be.

24   The producer and the director often have their own ideas about how the actor should look. I feel the objective of the performer is to try to appear as the director wants, and I am there to make this tangible. For example in 1954 when Alfred Lunt directed *Ondine* in which Audrey Hepburn played the title role, Mr. Lunt, his wife Lynn Fontanne, and Miss Hepburn all had conflicting ideas about makeup. In the end, to make Miss Hepburn into an ethereal water nymph we came up with a cap of gold hair to interlace with her own so that she would not have to color her hair. Tilted eyes and a slight, greenish hue to her makeup made her appear very much of another world.

Only through the practical experience of trial and error, based on certain fundamental and practical facts, can you become proficient in the art of makeup. It cannot be mastered over night.

Men's Makeup

Even though the young have liberated the American male and he now has a freedom of dress long denied him; even though there is a trend toward hair styling and coloring,

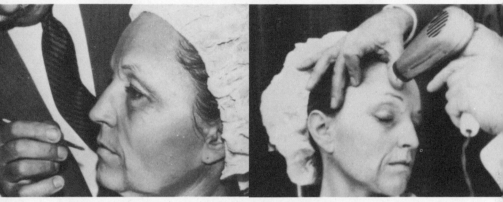

3—intense lip color is removed; 4—designer Senz dries a latex surface to achieve a wrinkled skin texture;

colognes, and more colorful clothing, a man's makeup should still be executed to look like there is none at all.

The kind and amount of light used has a great deal of bearing on the makeup. Dressing room light is not the same as stage light. A flesh tone face will wash out under red and yellow lights—you need to use something more opaque and warmer in tone. A pale-skinned man with a heavy beard can look like a ghost, unless he uses more opaque makeup to reflect light. Then, makeup that was right for the first show must be reconsidered when it goes on the road where lighting will be changing continuously.

25

One cannot assume that an indiscriminate use of makeup will establish the performer or will help in changing his face to the character he wishes to portray. Otto Preminger once called me in to consult on his makeup precisely because he did not want to be bothered with too much 'hokus pokus.' He was opening in *Margin for Error* which he also directed. I suggested a crewcut, a monocle, a scar on his cheek, and a cutaway with wing collars. Preminger sent me a wire after

5—*wig in place, he washes down excess powder and gives the skin surface a less matted look; 6—surveying the finished product;*

the opening, saying: 'The show is a great success and I promise you that your scar will be the most famous scar in America.' I was also called in by Garson Kanin to consult with Joseph Schildkraut, who did not want to spend a lot of time arranging a bald pate. Instead, I suggested that he shave his head for his part of the father in *The Diary of Anne Frank.*

Every production has its unique problems and own solutions. The makeup artist has to understand the history of the part, the period of the play, what people wore, and what they did with their hair. I worked closely with Richard Kiley, the first *Man of La Mancha* to select the right moustache, beard, and hair for his Quixote image.

It is also important that an actor first acquaint himself with all the various expressions and muscular movements, and then apply makeups to substitute his own expression with one more suitable to the part he is playing.

7—the youthful Peggy Senz as an aged woman.

Different Media

The medium you are working in demands differing makeup techniques. What is suitable for the stage is not right for motion pictures, or television. I think motion picture makeup is the most difficult. You have to be so exacting, so fine and delicate. In the early days of color filming, Technicolor would not allow their name or equipment to be used unless I went along to do the right makeup for color. Every line, every edge can be seen when projected on the big screen. Blending of colors and the selection of hair must appear much more natural than on the stage. With stage makeup you can exaggerate—it has to carry farther.

In the theatre today, all too often young people arrive to work in their chosen field, competent in their performing

27

ability, but without the least idea of how to do a professional, straight makeup. In cases where they have been taught some makeup in high schools and college drama departments, often the techniques are heavy-handed or a little old fashioned. Makeup has changed and advanced to such a degree that some university people are not fully equipped to give the most up-to-date information or instruction.

Some Suggestions

It would be impossible to discuss the entire field of makeup and its advances to date, but there is some basic information that should make the subject more accessible to students of drama. Many brands of theatrical makeup in unlimited colors and shades are on the market today. They come in jars, sticks, pancakes, and press powders, containing a high percentage of pigment for better skin coverage. The experienced actors, with a few basic colors—yellow, red, brown, black, and white—can obtain many by mixing all the shades and hues he needs. I, personally, prefer the thinner pan sticks and pancakes, which are simpler to apply and quite satisfactory.

For the student, a makeup kit should contain, besides the colors mentioned above, two fundamental colors—a light pink used for a woman's complexion and dark pink for middle-aged men and women. It should also contain six lining colors: light brown, blue-gray, light and dark red, white and black; derma wax for building up the nose; nose putty; eyebrow brushes; flat shading brushes; pencils in brown, maroon and black; sealer; a little gray hair; adhesive for the hair; solvent; liquid latex; plastic sponges; scissors; combs; hair whitener; a powder puff; tissues and cold cream. In addition, a woman's kit should also contain false eyelashes and lipsticks.

The makeup artist can be likened to a portrait painter. Without a purpose he just uses paints on a canvas, hoping to complete a portrait. Unless he has a plan and knows what to do with color and shading, it could all be futile. Beware of a heavy hand—it can spoil the illusion of character created by good acting.

It may only be skin deep, but makeup creates the images that help sell votes, critics, and ticket buyers.

The time-consuming process that elaborate character makeups require is too extravagant to repeat night after night for each theatre performance, or day after day for each film shooting. Short cuts have to be found. Makeup prosthetics—those artificial elements that are added to the face to build up more sculptural makeups—are the prefabrication shortcut that has grown most steadily in use. They also refine coarseness. The new materials available for making prosthetics lightweight and flexible and the methods of constructing and attaching those elements to actors' faces and hands have produced a separate specialization for makeup artists. Although his work represents a full range of makeup activities, Dick Smith is known among his compeers as an expert in makeup prosthetics. He describes the steps in designing and fabricating the elements—first making a life mask, then a character mask, then the latex sculptured pieces; next he describes putting makeup over those elements. His method for this facial sculpture and painting is meticulous. It is also a highly complicated, time and patience consuming, three-dimensional process that Dick Smith does not recommend for non-professionals. His techniques show the heights of makeup professionalism that an experienced master craftsman can aspire to.

Dick Smith became fascinated with makeup while studying at Yale and in 1945 was hired by NBC as the first staff makeup

29

artist in television. *During 14 years as head of the NBC makeup department and two seasons with David Susskind's Talent Associates, his work on television specials included: Jose Ferrer's "Cyrano de Bergerac," "The Barretts of Wimpole Street" with Katherine Cornell, "Victoria Regina" with Claire Bloom, "The Moon and Sixpence" with Sir Laurence Olivier, "Medea" with Dame Judith Anderson, "Don Quixote" with Lee J. Cobb, and "The Devil and Dan'l Webster" with Edward G. Robinson and David Wayne. In 1961 he went to Hollywood and worked in films— "Requiem for a Heavyweight," "It's a Mad, Mad, Mad, Mad World"—and in 1967 returned to television for "The Diary of Anne Frank"; "Soldier in Love" with Jean Simmons, Claire Bloom, and Keith Mitchell; "The Strange Case of Dr. Jekyll and Mr. Hyde" with Jack Palance; and a host of other shows. His work in the theatre includes: "Baker Street," "Wait Until Dark," "Do I Hear a Waltz," "The Unknown Soldier," "Walking Happy," "Dear World," "Zorba," and "The Soldiers." Recently he consulted on the films, "Midnight Cowboy," "Me, Natalie," "Little Big Man," and "Who is Harry Kellerman and Why is He Saying Those Terrible Things About Me?" and "The Godfather."*

The following was first published in "Theatre Crafts" in September, 1970

A variety of different molds was used by Dick Smith to create the makeup for Hal Holbrook's televised version of "Mark Twain Tonight."

Construction of Famous Faces

an interview with Dick Smith   31

THEATRE CRAFTS: Dick, you've been involved in make-up for television, movies, and the theatre; what would you say are the main characteristics of those three fields and how does makeup for them differ?

DICK SMITH: For many years, when I was just doing TV, I heard the movie guys say, 'Films are much harder than TV, you've got it easy.' Then, when I started in movies, I discovered that I actually had it easier in films. I could get away with a lot more in my complicated makeups.

TC: You mean that films were less exacting?

DS: That's right. On TV, errors and little mistakes show up more.

TC: That's interesting because most people feel that films, by virtue of the very size of the projected image, demand a greater care and skill in make-up.

DS: In films, say in a tight close-up where you have a full head shot, there are all kinds of tricks that can be used to diffuse the image just a little. The cameraman has a whole selection of little lenses that he can use to take some of the sharpness out of the focus.

TC: You mean they don't use those diffusion techniques in TV?

DS: Correct. And through the last ten years, television has been developing and now a TV camera is as sharp, in many ways, as a film camera. They have a great ability to show fine detail. If you have a full head on the TV screen you can pick up every little pore—even the net of a wig.

TC: Even though the image is so much larger on a movie screen?

DS: People are fooled by that. In reality, the size of the image you see in the movie theatre is usually in the same proportion to your distance from the screen as the television screen is from your chair at home. And don't forget, in the movies that image you're seeing is blown up from a small piece of film—that, too, contributes to the diffusion of the image.

32

TC: How does makeup for the theatre differ?

DS: There, as you know, you exaggerate. That's the fun part about theatre makeup. It's the one place where you can really paint. You can't do that in films or TV. You can get fantastic illusions with chiaroscuro. Just by painting with grease paints, you can make someone's eyelids look as big as half a golf ball. (That's what I tried to do for Angela Lansbury in "Dear World" to suggest her madness.)

TC: But this painting is not really what you are best known for in theatre makeup, is it?

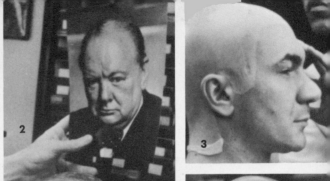

Basil Langton's photographs (these pages) record the construction of John Colicos' makeup as Winston Churchill in Hochhuth's "Soldiers." For step-by-step description, see text.

DS: No. The best way to understand both the kind of makeup I do and the way I work is to follow one of them step by step in photographs. Really the most complicated one was turning John Colicos into Winston Churchill for Hochhuth's "Soldiers," which ran in Canada, in New York for a short while, and then in London.

1. Here's what John Colicos really looks like.

2. At the wig maker, I am making a pattern for the thin wig that Colicos is to wear. The material is like a saran wrap—you put it over the head and then run tape over it until you get the shape of the man's head. (It's a traditional thing the wig makers use.) Then you draw on it the outline of the hair you want.

3. To prepare Colicos for the casting of his head and face—first of all you put on (usually not very carefully) a plastic cap. This is just to cover his hair.

4. To cast his head you use alginate, which dentists use to cast teeth. It is a powder that you mix with water; remains liquid for a while and then jells into a rubbery gelatin-like material.

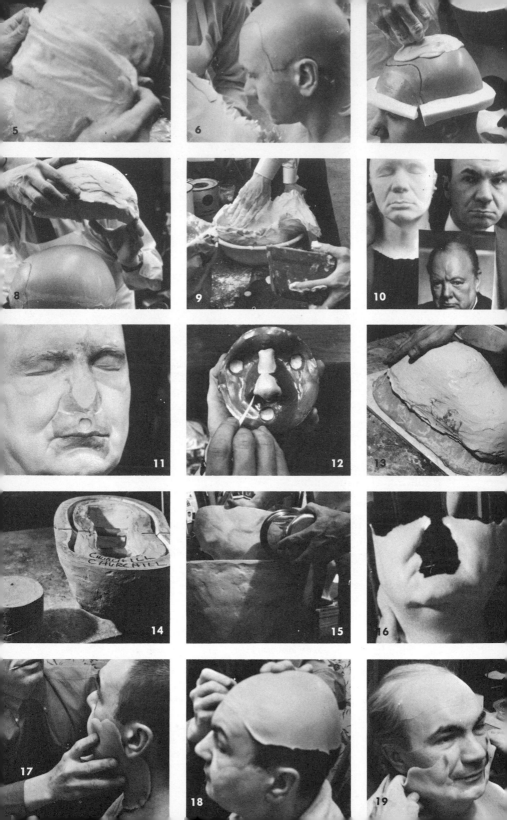

5. Over that, you put plaster bandages—like the ones doctors make casts out of. This supports that flexible alginate material, and both those layers then become a mold.

6. The plaster bandage is what we call a mother mold—it supports this soft inner mold, which now comes off. I even put the marks of his hair line on with indelible pencil so that it comes out in the mold.

7. I also cast the top of his head with just plain plaster.

8. It comes off and right away makes a mold so I can make rubber pates that will go on top of Colicos' head, underneath the wig, to make him look bald.

9. Then you put plaster inside that mold of the face.

10. Here is John Colicos, his life mask which comes out of that mold we just made, and a photograph of what he is to become—Winston Churchill.

11. Next I model over Colicos' life mask the face of Churchill, so that I now know where his face must be added to. In this photograph you can see that I have cut off the nose and also shaved the lower lip. This is to make it easier to work with. The hole is what we call a key—a place for the mold to lock into the correct position.

12. Here you can see three keys. This is the nose, ready to be cast. The white is a white clay, and the rest of the face is covered with a darker clay.

13. To cast the face of Churchill, plaster is poured over the face.

14. Here is the complete mold of the face and nose, made over the Churchill model. The inner part is Colicos' life mask. When the clay that was sculpted on Colicos' face is removed it leaves spaces between the life mask of Colicos and the Churchill he is to be.

15. The next step is to pour foam latex (rather like beaten up whipped cream) into the bottom mold, and push the head (Colicos' life mask) back into the mold so that the foam latex fills up the spaces where the clay had been added. Then I bake it in an oven to cure it.

35

The finished product—
John Colicos as
Winston Churchill (right).

16. The result is a foam latex piece like this; the cheeks, neck, chin, and nose are done the same way.

17. This piece of foam latex can be fitted to Colicos' face. The inside fits his own face exactly, and the outside has the appearance of Winston Churchill.

18. Here I am applying the rubber bald pate, which goes on before the wig.

19. John is trying on the piece.

20. Nearing completion.

21. The finished product—John Colicos as Winston Churchhill.

36

DS: There's one step that I have left out. The foam latex pieces have no color. So the entire mask must be extensively made up to make it look human. You cover the whole mask with a neutral color—what we call rubber mask grease paint. It's a thick paint with a castor oil base.

TC: Why castor oil?

DS: Because that's the one oil which can be used over rubber without turning color. Then over this you add colors like reds and browns to give it the illusion of the mottled coloring that most faces have. After you add reds, then you do things like liver spots, and make little dots hither and yon to break up that flat tone.

TC: Well you don't stay around to do this same makeup for a performer every night of the show, do you?

DS: No, I teach the actors how to apply it themselves.

TC: How do you go about that?

DS: The usual procedure is that I first show the performer. Then they put it on while I'm there, and I correct it until they're reasonably confident they can do it themselves. A key thing is to keep the makeup as simple and organized as possible so that the performer *can* do it himself. You don't do all the little fine touches you might if you were applying the makeup all the time yourself.

TC: How does a performer remember where everything goes —especially all those dots of color?

DS: When I set someone up—after we have established the make-up—then I do a sketch that diagrams where all the colors go. The performer often lays on makeup from this diagram until he is confident.

TC: Where do all the ingredients come from?

DS: Theoretically, actors are supposed to have their own makeup kits. But they don't. Rather than give someone a shopping list in those last critical days before an opening, and have them worrying about getting all the stuff, I usually buy it and charge it to the production, then label all the ingredients for their particular makeup.

TC: Could you have done these stage makeups the same way for television or films?

DS: In some ways they would not have to be altered. For instance I did a makeup for Milton Berle in Herb Gardener's "The Goodbye People" that could have been used for films. But it would have meant that the pieces must be put on and blended in much more carefully. Then after the pieces are in place you spray a little coat of liquid latex over the edges so it's like a skin over the whole face. And the coloring and stippling of the mask requires more care and time. Berle's makeup for theatre might take 45 minutes to apply, and for the films it would take two hours.

TC: You've also been called in to transform a stage make-up into something suitable for television, haven't you?

37

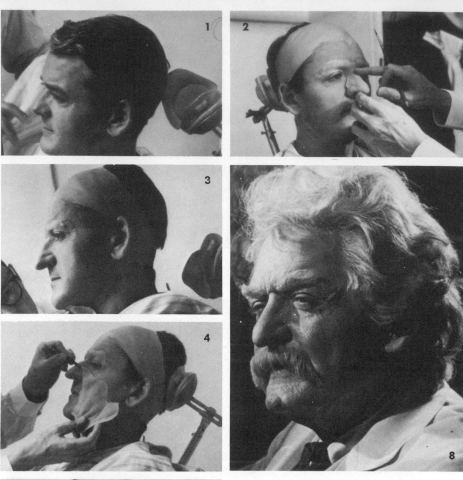

1—Hal Holbrook waiting to be made up for the television version of "Mark Twain Tonight". 2—Plastic bald forehead, eyebrow, and lid pieces in place and application of the nose. 3—Affixing the dewlap. 4—Gluing on the cheek pieces. 5—Attaching the chin. 6—Stippling and coloring the face. 7—Putting the wig in place. 8—Recreated, the creator of Tom Sawyer and Huck Finn ready for a public appearance.

DS: Yes, when Hal Holbrook did his "Mark Twain Tonight" on television.

TC: But Holbrook had already developed his own makeup for the stage.

DS: Yes, and what he did for the stage is beautiful, very well done—but after all it is only an illusion. It was highlights and shadows painted on to simulate age. For television and films, in order to make something look realistic, it has to be three-dimensional. So I was called in to redo the entire makeup, to create an honest 70 year old man with a face that would have every little wrinkle, every little pore and that would move.

TC: In reality, you redesigned the whole thing?

DS: Yes, but I spent a lot of time trying to find the image of Mark Twain that was closest to Hal Holbrook. We did three tests, and each time we refined the makeup again. I actually used Hal's life mask to do a sculpture of the makeup that enabled me to see just what had to be done, even to the extent of determining the size, length and thickness of the wig and moustache.

TC: In the theatre how do lighting and changes in lighting affect your make-up and the colors you plan to use?

DS: Well, it's not all that fine. For example, if you're doing an old age makeup you know pretty well that certain colors are going to come across in average stage lighting. If the lighting changes from scene to scene you can't change the makeup all the time so you try for a happy medium. You try the colors that you know from experience usually work, and then if under the lighting the makeup comes off a little too red or yellow or whatever, you have a point of reference to adjust.

TC: In the time that you have been doing makeup have there been major changes in materials that have noticeably changed the profession?

DS: There are of course new materials both for straight and character makeups. New materials may ease certain problems, but it all remains basically the same.

TC: Foam latex seems to be basic to a lot of the work you do.

DS: Well, foam latex has been around since the 30's—the movie of "The Wizard of Oz" made use of a lot of foam

39

latex. It still has not been replaced by another material because they have not found anything as flexible and elastic.

TC: Do they use a lot of foam latex in the theatre?

DS: Not usually because for the theatre it is relatively expensive. That mask that I did for John Colicos' role of Winston Churchill was unusual. Something like that costs about $250 a mask and they don't generally last more than two weeks before they have to be replaced. Of course, it's different for TV and films—not only do they really demand the three-dimensionality of the foam latex, but they can usually afford it as well.

TC: Are there any problems in working with foam latex?

DS: Well it is a tricky thing, and because it is hard to work with and expensive, it is not the kind of material that I would recommend for amateurs. Also, you must remove the latex pieces with soap and water—an oily solvent dissolves it into the worst kind of glue.

TC: Are you able to use cosmetics designed for regular street wear?

DS: Yes. For straight makeups some of them come in handy. For example, I used some of the gel makeups in "Midnight Cowboy" to make Dustin Hoffman look unwashed and grimy. The advantage of this material is that it is very believable because it is completely transparent.

TC: Each new makeup you do just by virtue of the character you're creating, the actor being used, or the demands of the stage or the TV and movie camera must create new problems to solve.

40

Jack Palance's makeup for "The Strange Case of Dr. Jekyll and Mr. Hyde" created a believable transformation.

The real Godfrey Cambridge (left) was made up as a white man (right) in "The Watermelon Man," for which Dick Smith created the original test makeup.

DS: Sure. For example, I turned Godfrey Cambridge into a white man when he tested for the movie "Watermelon Man." He had to wear a wig that would have been impossible to glue on to that greasy make-up—so, I formulated something like a flesh tone paint that we used instead.

TC: Hal Holbrook wore a white suit as Twain, didn't he?

DS: Yes, and he was always putting his hands in his pockets! That rubber mask grease paint he had on is one of the messiest things, so I had to eliminate it entirely on his neck and hands. I came up with a mixture of an acrylic paint and latex that would not rub off. The trick was to get a color that matched the makeup exactly.

41

TC: You also designed old crone masks for three girls in the musical "Zorba," didn't you?

DS: The trick there was to give them something that would be rugged and yet allow a certain amount of movement. Also the changes had to be very quick. I came up with a combination of my foam latex material and pure latex (which is the kind of thing that Halloween masks are made of)—it's quite tough. I made the masks out of a layer of pure latex and backed up the jowly sections with foam latex. To make the changes easier the mask was fastened with Velcro closures.

For an episode of television's "Dark Shadows" Dick Smith turned Jonathan Frid (left) into the aged vampire, Barnabas (right).

TC: What did you do about Fritz Weaver's makeup when he played Sherlock Holmes?

DS: What he was mainly doing was quick-change disguises— some of them were done on stage. They had to be done fast and every night, so there was a minimum of actual application of makeup and a maximum of devices that could be stuck on and taken off. They were rugged and designed to last for months. There was another problem there—Fritz Weaver is allergic to spirit gum, so we used a two-sided tape under all the hair pieces, and he pretended to be gluing them on.

42

TC: You've worked in all the fields of makeup now, which one do you prefer?

DS: Television—because I can see my work immediately on the monitor. I was brought up that way, and I have never gotten used to the delay of films.

TC: Where does one learn this art of makeup, and then get into the field?

DS: Well, that's difficult. It is such a small field and there is not a neat way to get in. Right now the only way is through an apprenticeship. But they are limited. And, well, you really learn makeup by doing it—by experimenting with it—that's what I did.

*Changing an actor's face from one charac-
ter to a markedly different one during a
single performance is professional challenge enough for a makeup designer.
Changing two actors into eight characters
during a single performance—and in split-
second intervals—is a hurdle of the highest
professionalism. It requires a designer to
think about systems of makeup application,
to plan procedures of timing and order,
rather than concentrating on the craft of
what to apply. Which is quicker: to put dirt
makeup on or to take it off, to put beauty-
fashion makeup on or take it off? Which is
quicker: to comb in a new hair style or to
remove a wig? The answer is that if what
an actor puts on takes so many more steps
and so much more time than what he takes
off, then a makeup designer should question
the usual procedure and consider reversing
the order.*

*Joseph Cranzano reveals how he arrived
at a methodology to skim over these hurdles
in flying style for the production of "The
Apple Tree" in 1967. "The Apple Tree" was
the first Broadway show to list the billing
"Makeup Created By." It was also the first
Broadway show for which Joseph Cranzano
designed all the makeup. A commercial artist before he chanced an apprenticeship in
television makeup, Joseph Cranzano designed makeup for NBC-TV from 1959 to
1967 and then launched himself on a free-
lance basis. For television he contributed*

43

makeup to such shows as "DuPont Show of the Week," "That Was The Week That Was," "ABC Stage '67," and "The Bell Telephone Hour." More recently he designed makeup for television specials on George Gershwin, Julie Andrews and Carol Burnett at Philharmonic Hall, and "Dames at Sea." Every year for the last six, he has designed the makeup for the Tony Awards. On the stage, his makeup has been seen in "Her First Roman," "Plaza Suite," "Two By Two," "No, No, Nanette," "Twigs," "Scratch," and "Sugar."

The following article was first published in "Theatre Crafts" in the March/April issue, 1967.

44

Quick-Change Makeup

by Joseph Cranzano

When I was called to make up Barbara Harris for some still photographs to be used in conjunction with a new musical she was in rehearsal for, *The Apple Tree*, I never expected what would develop from such a routine assignment. I was called by Ernie Adler, who had been contracted by Stuart Ostrow, the producer, to create the hairstyles for the show.

At the photo studio, I found Ernie and Barbara Harris already waiting. Barbara was sitting silently, in sort of a heap, looking exhausted after a difficult day of rehearsal. For the photos, she was to look like a composite of Marilyn Monroe and Jayne Mansfield. In short, the epitome of the Hollywood sex goddess. That didn't present any particular problem, since a makeup artist spends most of his professional life making women look as beautiful as they possibly can.

As I started to work, with Ernie looking on, Mike Nichols, the show's director, arrived. Realizing he could do very little at this point, Mike asked how long it would be before we would be ready. Ernie and I estimated about an hour and a half for the makeup and hair. Mike, having a friend with him, decided to go out to dinner.

Joseph Cranzano designed makeup for Barbara Harris in Act III of "The Apple Tree" that effected a quick change from Ella (bottom left) to Passionella (top left). In Act II she was madeup as Princess Barbára (top right), and in Act I she played Eve (bottom right).

After about fifteen minutes, we started to see the effects of what I was attempting to create. But Barbara remained relatively silent and Ernie watched intently, while I continued working. Then, as things started happening, she began to interject some ideas of her own. Pretty soon the three of us were working together and becoming very enthusiastic about the project. Finally, with the makeup completed, Ernie put a styled, platinum-blonde wig on Barbara and the result was breathtaking.

It's really hard to decide whether the makeup made Barbara, or Barbara made the makeup. I'd like to believe it was half of both. In any case, we were thrilled with result.

As if on cue, Mike Nichols returned. I remember him looking into the dressing-room, seeing Barbara (who had changed into her costume), pausing for a moment, and asking timidly, "Barbara?"

The Passionella Problem

During the photo session, Mike came over to me and said, "You know, Joe, we have a makeup problem in this show you might help us solve. Barbara has to change *from* something into this," he indicated her posing as Passionella. She's going to be Ella, a little chimney sweep. A plain girl, very dirty and quite grubby looking, with no makeup at all. Then, she's got to effect a quick change and become Passionella."

I answered that it could be done, and asked if he had any idea of how long a time lapse there would be. I remember asking if we had at least five minutes, realizing it had taken Ernie and me all of an hour and a half to get her ready for the photo session.

47

"I can tell you exactly," he said. At that point he started to read the script in his mind, while he timed it on his watch. All I could hear was: "Ella sits down . . . blah blah blah. Plunk plunk . . . she crosses . . . ba boom pow . . . There you go Joe, you'll have 45 seconds."

I can't remember at all what I said, at that point, if I said anything. But I know I told myself—impossible. What can you do in 45 seconds? She has to come out of one costume and into a tight sequined gown, out of one wig into another. And she has to have a complete makeup change too.

All I had were visions of a Mack Sennett comedy with arms, hands, heads, legs, and bodies flying in every direction. Which was exactly the case, the first time we tried it in Boston.

More Quick Changes

There were two more picture sessions to complete the Passionella photos necessary for the show. I discovered then that these shots would be used in the show as rear-screen projections. I also learned that *The Apple Tree* was composed of three, one-act musicals and that Barbara and her co-star Alan Alda were to play eight different people. In the first act, Barbara was to play Eve in "Adam and Eve," and in act II, the ferocious princess Barbára in "The Lady or the Tiger." However, in the third act she would play two characters: Ella and Passionella. In the first act, Alan would be Adam; and in the second act, Captain Sanjar. He, too, would play two characters in act III: Flip, the Prince Charming, and a timid banker, George L. Brown.

After the last photo session, Mike asked me if I'd join the company to work out the makeup. Of course, I accepted enthusiastically.

Although I knew the entire show would be a challenge, there was no point in thinking about anything else until I had solved the Passionella-Ella problem. I really didn't have 45 seconds for a makeup change. Because all of the other elements, the costume changes and the wig change for instance, had to be accounted for. All in all, I figured I would have, at the most, 20 seconds to effect the change. Nobody can be made up in 20 seconds. In fact, I would be lucky to powder her down in 20 seconds. Obviously, all the makeup had to be on and it would be a matter of taking something off.

I came to the conclusion she had to be made up as Passionella first. That is, I would put on her complete Passionella makeup, then obliterate it and create Ella over that. My biggest problem was, how to cover Passionella's makeup and not destroy it. Or, how to take off the make-up which creates Ella and leave the makeup for Passionella.

48

At every opportunity during the next two weeks, I tried every approach I could think of, using myself as a testing ground. Because it seemed a complicated problem, I tried complicated approaches. I was having little success—until I found the simple way of doing it.

The Solution

Of course, everything seems easy when you find the answer, but the solution for this problem was simplicity itself. After I finished the Passionella makeup, all I had to do was use a flesh colored powder to cover the entire face. By doing this, what remained was a blank face and two large eyes. All that was required now was the heavy application of dirt, Ella's basic look. Of course, it wasn't an ordinary dirt preparation, but one I devised for this quick change. It was a mixture of water-soluble jelly and black powder. When prepared properly, it can be removed from the face with a few gentle swipes of a damp sponge. In this case, the process of removing the dirt also removed the powder, revealing the Passionella make-up completely intact. The only thing left for Barbara was to apply a little lip gloss to restore the lustre and color to her lipstick, which was muted by the application of powder. Her Passionella eye makeup was no problem, because strands of her Ella wig covered up most of it, so it wasn't fully seen until she was wearing her Passionella wig. The whole process took about 15 seconds and her makeup transformation was complete.

During Performance

Here's what takes place during her change: the first thing that happens is that her Ella wig is yanked off. The wardrobe lady zips her out of her Ella dress. I grab one arm, clean that off with two or three swipes of a big sponge, while on the other side the hairdresser is doing the same thing with the other arm. As soon as Barbara gets one arm free, I hand her a face sponge and she proceeds to wipe off her Ella face. (It's faster for her to do it than one of us.) During that time, of course, the hairdresser is putting on the big blonde wig. Barbara is getting into her gown, and the wardrobe lady is helping her into her shoes.

The first time we did the change, it took us about two minutes. Everything was flying and nothing was happening.

49

This was simply because we had not perfected each single step each of us was to perform during the change. The second time wasn't much better. And the third time, which was dress-rehearsal, we may have been 10 seconds late. But being 10 seconds late, after you've gotten your cue, leaves a gap and the excitement of the effect can die in those 10 seconds. The first time we got it right was the first time we played before an audience. And it has worked every time since. Now, it has gotten to a point, where Barbara has about six seconds to check her makeup.

The Other Character Changes

Ordinarily, the Eve makeup in the first act would not have posed any particular problems. All she had to be was soft and beautiful—or, as Mike Nichols had put it, "a creation of God." Yet Mike wanted no illusions of make-up, and finally it was refined to a point, where all the elements and definitions necessary to carry the look were there, but no makeup was apparent. Eve looks soft and natural. The makeup is all there, but you are not aware of it.

For the character Barbára in the second act, the makeup was entirely another concept. The point there was to make her look intense—exotic. Of course, this required bolder strokes, but again I tried to keep the awareness of the makeup to a minimum.

The makeup changes for each act had to be done during intermissions, but there was a race against time to effect the change from one character to another. For this reason, and for the first time on Broadway, a makeup artist was present at every performance.

To make the change from Eve to Barbára, between the acts, I was able to work directly over the Eve makeup. That saved some time. However, in changing from Barbára to Ella-Passionella, between the second and third act, the change-over required washing and drying the whole face, costume changes, wig changes, and pretty soon our working time for applying the Ella-over-Passionella double makeup was down to seconds again.

Luckily, Alan Alda's makeup changes were less complicated. For his Adam, we got the naiveté Mike wanted just by emphasizing the eyes. The rest of the face was done in a basic foundation.

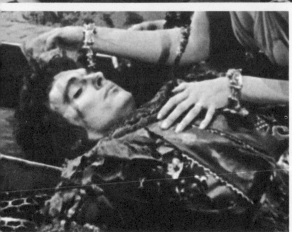

Designer Cranzano made up
Alan Alda as Adam in Act I of
"The Apple Tree" (above left)
and as Captain Sanjar in Act II
(bottom left). In Act III he designed a quick change from
"Flip" (above right) to the
timid banker George L. Brown.

In the second act, Alan becomes Captain Sanjar, the hardened, ascetic warrior returning from battle. But this change didn't present any specific problems and was made easily with the basic techniques of shading and highlighting.

In the third act, Alan plays Flip, the Prince Charming, and George L. Brown, a timid banker. Flip is a cool, motorcycle-riding, leather-jacketed hippy with long, wild hair and dirty fingernails (which he says make a person real). To get the pale, blank look, usually associated with this type of character, we decided to use no make-up at all. It worked beautifully.

To effect his change from Flip to George L. Brown, Alan had his hair slicked down and parted before he put the Flip wig on. So all he did was to take off the wig, put on a pair of horn-rimmed glasses, get into a suit, and he became the timid banker.

I have often heard performers talk about how different theatre is from every other form of entertainment. Now I know what they mean. The immediacy of being ready, getting changes perfected, and hearing the response from the audience, is unique. *The Apple Tree* will always remain my introduction to that excitement and fulfillment.

Non-makeup and minimal makeup are increasingly a part of the non-illusionist or "realistic" theatre of today—those movements called Environmental Theatre and the New Theatre, which are in direct juxtaposition or confrontation to the traditional theatre of naturalism and illusion. Those new directions aim at involving their audiences more actively by eliminating the distinctions between actors and audiences, by having performers appear without makeup as if in real-life, among other means. It is paradoxical, therefore, that one branch of illusionist theatre—television—which attempts to recreate the actual appearances of reality as much as any medium, should also tend toward minimal makeup or non-makeup. That irony may be a key to the future. When television makeup designers crusade against the heaviness and artificiality of makeup in the theatre, as they frequently do, they are challenging traditional theatre, not Environmental Theatre. Yet their goal is an extreme of naturalism, of creating the illusion of actual street makeup.

For a popular daytime television serial, makeup designers have interesting challenges, as CBS-TV makeup designer Phil Edelson and hair stylist Ted Zane reveal. One challenge is the daily schedule, which requires staggered phasing of applying makeup on actors, since they are called at various times for rehearsal before the

53

actual taping. Another is the involvement of actors in their own makeup decisions and in the subsequent changes in those decisions. Serial stories require that television audiences see consistent and unchanging characters. So makeup designers must find ways to keep makeups consistent throughout seasonal changes when actors get summer suntans or winter pasty faces. How to compensate for these changes and for changes of lighting are some of the insights that television designers can share with colleagues in other media.

Phil Edelson has created the makeup for numerous CBS-TV productions, including the "Gary Moore Show," the "Jackie Gleason Show," and for 14 years, the "Ed Sullivan Show." He also served as makeup consultant to individual actors and has worked on several Broadway and Off-Broadway productions.

Ted Zane, born in Greece, came to this country and studied at the Ingrid School of Hair Design and Brooklyn College. He is currently hair designer for CBS-TV, where he worked with the "Ed Sullivan Show" for its last four years. His film credits include the hair designs for "Goodbye Columbus" and "Funny Girl."

The following article by "Theatre Crafts" contributing editor Glenn M. Loney, whose biographical sketch appears on page 102, was first published in "Theatre Crafts," January/February 1972.

54

Getting to Look Like Yourself for TV

by Glenn M. Loney

It may look like real life in your living room, but that illusion is not easily come by at the CBS-TV daytime epic, *Love is a Many Splendored Thing*. The craft is familiar— it's makeup. But how are the familiar stage makeup techniques adapted to a different performance medium—that of television? During a recent, pre-show makeup session, Phil Edelson, the makeup designer, and Ted Zane, hair stylist, commented on their work and how different time schedules, lighting conditions, long runs, and close-up camera work in television affect their crafts.

It was a big day for the cast. Judson Laire, the senior citizen charmer of the show, was getting married to Diana Douglas. For those among the nearly eight million fans who watch this show five days a week (2–2:30 EST), of course, those performers are more intimately known as Dr. Will Donnelly and Lily Chernak. Taking its title from Han

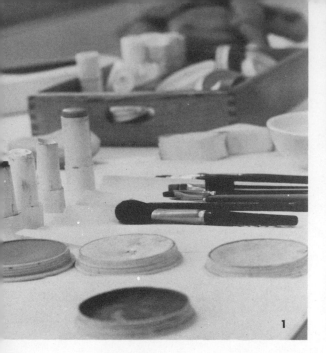

Suyin's novel, this serial has been on the air since September 18, 1967. Its scene is San Francisco, and the episodes are engineered around the lives of three families there: the Donnellys, the Elliotts, and the Chernaks.

Coordinating the Time Schedules

A wedding is a major event in real life, and at the CBS studios—a remodeled dairy plant on West 57th Street in New York—it requires more coordination, faster work, and more concentration than usual. This is especially true for Phil Edelson and Ted Zane. The TV nuptial manages to bring together more of the show's cast than is customarily on set for daily episodes. That means careful planning and swift, deft application to get everyone made up in time for the morning dress rehearsal, and then ready for actual color taping after a brief lunch break.

By 9 AM, Edelson has already been at his makeup table for some time. Several actors, their faces glowing with a panstick base, are trying out costumes for last minute adjustments. The base is quickly applied, and when they—or Edelson—have a free moment the makeup will be finished and powdered.

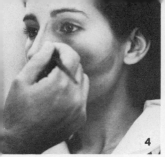

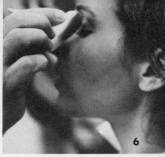

4 **5** **6**

*Phil Edelson's TV makeup table (1) has a
simple but comprehensive lineup of pansticks,
powders, eye shadows, pencils, and brushes of
varying sizes, shapes, and functions. Working
on actress Andrea Marcovicci, Edelson shades
the cheekbones using a rough-cut foam rubber
sponge (2, 3), shades the nose with a brush
(4), and blends the makeup base over the
shading on the cheeks (5), the eyelids (6), and
the neck (7).*

7

Later, downstairs on the studio stage, Edelson will re-
touch anything that needs to be adjusted to the lights and
settings. He works rapidly but gently, his super-fine, syn-
thetic sponges seeming barely to touch the face. Cut up
foam rubber mattress used as a sponge gives a finer effect,
Edelson feels, than natural sponge which he also uses.

"I call this gilding-the-lily hour," he says amiably. It is
a pleasant task he performs five days a week usually on
eight actors. The wedding today, however, is like a family
reunion and there are five women to be made up—not to
mention the necessary wigs and hair-do's which must also
be handled in very little time. "I have about an hour, after
the dress rehearsal for the hair," comments Ted Zane. "I
have to work fast."

Preparing for Closeup Camera Work

In answer to the question, "Are women more trouble to
make up than men?" Edelson comments: "Of course. We
don't do anything very involved here. Less is more. The
cameras work so very close to the performers that the kind
of makeup people often do for the stage looks ridiculous.
All those heavy 'character' lines may seem to blend into a

57

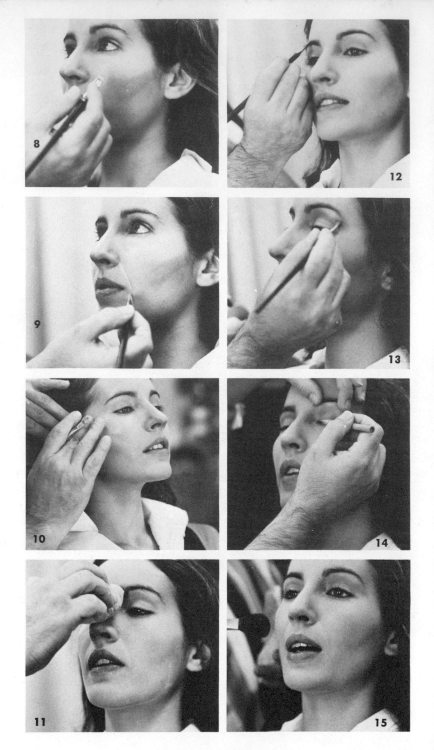

58

Designer Edelson next highlights cheekbones (8) nose wrinkles (9), and temples (10). With a natural sponge, he powders lightly (11), removes and sets the powder with a damp sponge, then pencils the brows (12), shades (13) and lines the eye (14), and powders lightly (15). The process transforms the actress into medical student Betsey Chernak, who, as Edelson comments, is a girl not very concerned with her looks (16).

smooth makeup for a theatre audience at twenty feet or more. But, not in the TV studio, under those bright lights. But, with women, it's basically the eye makeup that takes the most time. Applying the liners, the shadow, putting on false eye lashes, touching up the lashes with mascara. That's important to a woman's appearance."

Working on a face before him, Edelson gently powders down, then takes a sponge, dampens it, and removes the excess. Six inches away, no one could know the face had ever been powdered. Delicate brown shadows below the cheekbones make them seem more defined, but they have been so well blended that it is impossible to identify them as makeup. Two minutes ago, they were tiny tan triangles on either side of the face. Blended, they make the cheek less fleshed than it really is.

Edelson draws some contrast between TV and theatre. "I did the *Ed Sullivan Show* for fourteen years, with a crew of assistants of course. One time Hal Holbrook was going to be on doing a show like his Mark Twain, only about Abraham Lincoln. He is famous for doing his own makeup. The Twain job is supposed to take three hours for the stage. And, it is very good—for the theatre. But, you cannot do

59

that kind of makeup for TV. Those heavy lines may look fine from the balcony of the Shubert, but they are deadly on TV. They look grotesque. To make Holbrook look like the Lincoln he was playing on stage, the makeup had to be much less exaggerated on TV."

The Bright Lights of Television

"Of course, one reason for this minimal approach to makeup is the closeup camera work, but another is our lighting," he continues. "It is very different from the theatre's. It is very bright; it is seldom, if ever colored; and it is mostly from overhead. Front lighting and side lighting may be all right for the theatre, but in the TV studio, the lights have to be out of the way of the cameras. And, overhead is a fine place for them. Also, they don't want actors' shadows on the set. The result: the lighting tends to be very *flat*. That can distort a face, and I have to compensate for that in my makeup." He shrugs his shoulders, "But it's the nature of the beast, I have to work all that much more delicately, much more lightly."

Something else about lights is that it creates a problem with some actresses—the so-called "pretty face." "An actress may have been told how pretty she looks, and she thinks with a bit of general makeup she's ready to dazzle the public. But a pretty face doesn't always work on camera. Often it may be round, regular, attractive. But, it really doesn't have many features, or much character. Under those bright, flat studio lights, that round, little face will just disappear. It won't make any effect at all. Pretty faces usually require more subtle character lines than those faces which are stamped by nature—or experience."

In the same vein, Phil Edelson went on to talk about how actors respond to makeup. "Most actors like to have their makeup done for them, and not just because it's nice to sit back in the chair with your eyes closed and have someone fuss over you. But, there is a problem with other actors. It's an ego thing. They may think they know what their best features are—and they really don't. In trying to emphasize these features, they may actually be heightening something better left unnoticed. With some performers, it's almost an inner perversity that won't let them see what is best for their bone structure, their facial muscles, their skin, and hair coloring.

"In making actors up, I believe," says Edelson, "that you must 'Make the Punishment Fit the Crime.' By that, I mean the makeup must be right for the part. It doesn't necessarily have to make an actor or actress look marvelous. Not if the part doesn't call for it. But that's the ego thing again, they want to look good—no matter what.

"TV audiences," Edelson admits, don't want *real* realism. That's true. They wouldn't want to see an actress made up the way her character actually would look if she were just getting out of bed. No, the hair will be in place, if in curlers. The face will look good. Not like you'd spent the night turning and tossing and woke up all rumpled."

Using Color Effectively

"Everything," comments Edelson, "is coordinated to our set colors. And we avoid a wide range of colors. They would be too hard to work with under the bright lights. Of course skins are different in their hues. To avoid strong contrasts, I often have to bring one actor's skin color 'up' while I'm toning 'down' another's.

"When summer comes I have to work harder. For actors who tan heavily, I have to lighten the tone a lot. For those who get red, I put green all over the face. Green cancels out red. They make a gray, which is good for our kind of TV lighting. I also use green over scars, and birthmarks. It's not laid on; it is thin enough so that it combines with the red to make a grayish tone."

61

Working on Judson Laire, a courtly actor, Edelson shows how gray the skin-toned, Bob Kelly Makeup is. Laire's face is ruddy. The hearty color vanishes. Another actor, Vincent Baggetta has just recently shaved a heavy beard which left some redness. Edelson has to kill both the beard, and the red. This he does with a very light, but grayish flesh tone. When all traces of the beard's root have vanished, he then applies a darker skin tone.

On the makeup table is a range of Bob Kelly shades. "I use these because they have the gray tones that work for

TV. Of course, Max Factor is still used, but TV does require special shades. Kelly even has a range of tones for black actors. Still, black skin doesn't need as much makeup as white skin does. It's not washed out by the lights. It absorbs, rather than reflects. But you have to be careful, if you lighten black skin with makeup; it may look grayish and pasty. Some lighter skins have a lot of green and yellow in them. For those skins, you have to use bases which will warm up the color. When Vivian Leigh did *Tovarich* on Broadway, she wanted to look very fair. The color of the stage light was pink, and her "fair" makeup made her look chalky. So finally to get the right effect, a lavender makeup had to be worked out.

"Actually, TV makeups have started a lot of popular makeup fashions. So many women who watch the shows want to look like their screen favorites. I know eye makeups go all the way back to the Egyptians, but it was TV that encouraged the recent emphasis on eye liners. And pale lipsticks—those originated on TV."

Washing off the powder on another makeup job Edelson noted, "it sets better when you wash it. It doesn't leave that chalky look that you get from merely brushing it off. In the summertime, the water can help if there is a tendency to perspire.

"I use pancake sometimes because it gives a heavier cover. It also gives a flatter look which you want for age. For a younger makeup you work for more skin 'shine' or radiance. Pancake is better for people who may perspire a lot. With grease paint, the perspiration comes up under it and that's not good," Edelson explains. "With stage makeup, sweat can be a problem, too. It can turn the grease paint orange and you've got to watch out for cracks around the eyes, if you've put it on too heavy."

Hair and Wigs

If Phil Edelson has been slaving since 8 AM, Ted Zane has been having an easier time of it. His frantic period is just before actual taping, when the women's hair must be freed from their curlers and made to look lovely. "I have about four or five sets and comb outs every day. Maybe that's not so good for the hair, but secretaries do it." If

*A length of bandage around actress
Diana Douglas' own hair (1) provides a
firm foundation for Ted Zane to pin, fit
(2), and style the wig she wears for her
role as Lily Chernak (3).*

there is a courtroom scene, there may be more women's hair
to tend to, but extras don't get as much attention as the
featured players. Zane keeps the men in the cast in trim,
too. Every two weeks, each one gets a haircut from him.
Even for the men, there cannot be sudden, strange contrasts in hair length from one day to the next, or any following of mad impulses to get a new hair styling when it
is not called for, or prepared for in the script.

At present, there is only one wig wearer in the female
cast. Zane uses a length of ace bandage to wrap up Diana
Douglas' own hair. This holds it down flat, close to the head,
but it also gives a much needed surface to which the wig
can be fastened. "This way" he says, "I need only two hair-
pins to hold it," Zane explains. The fine wig lace is apparent

63

to the naked eye, but when covered with a fixative it becomes invisible.

Zane notes that if for some reason any woman in the show wants to change her own hair length, style or color, she has to get the producer's permission. She is under contract to play a certain role. If her hair suddenly is chopped off and dyed red that means the expense of providing a wig to make her look like her old TV self.

The Finishing Touches

Edelson and Zane have a special table for makeup on the stage. After watching a dress rehearsal on monitors, they often have small changes to make. Once costumes are on, makeup can be blended down to the neckline. If a light from above is bringing out an undesirable facial crease, a white line may be blended into it. If a performer's hands need some makeup, they get a coating. Such closeup work as hands playing the piano, writing a letter, cooking, or even a hand held pensively against the face, where it *must* match —all of these require special attention.

But, after all, it is an illusion, even when the camera is working so closely. You may have seen the wedding celebration. How were you to know that the furniture and the settings, closeup, are not nearly so elegant or expensive as they look. Even in TV there is still room for such illusion. With Phil Edelson's makeup and Ted Zane's hair-do's, however, the wizardry that is there, is so cleverly blended into the straight makeup that those people really look off camera rather like their video-selves.

*In the first five years of "Theatre Crafts"
publication, television was improved technically to such a degree—especially in its
capacity to produce accurate colors and to
transmit clear images—that the art of television makeup had to be revised almost
totally. Whereas everyday street makeup
seemed a model for natural television
makeup some five years earlier, by 1972
television designers considered street
makeup almost as heavy-handed as traditional makeup for the theatre. This updated view of the craft was discussed and
demonstrated in detail at a seminar that
should become, in itself, a model of procedure for teaching makeup to large groups.*

*Lee Baygan and Bob Kelly, who conducted
the seminar, are both respected makeup
technicians. Lee Baygan is chief of makeup
for NBC-TV in New York, where he has
refined the craft over the past 17 years;
there he daily supervises makeup for TV
shows originating in New York. He has
been responsible for such recent television
productions as a 1972 N.E.T. production
of "Antigone" starring Genevieve Bujuold
and Stacey Keach and in 1973 the Joseph
Papp-produced A. J. Antoon-directed
"Much Ado About Nothing." For a
biographical sketch of the other seminar
leader, Bob Kelly, see page 228. The following report, written by Patricia J.
MacKay, whose biographical sketch appears on p. 91, was first published in
"Theatre Crafts," October 1972.*

65

Film and TV Makeup

a seminar with Lee Baygan

In and around Rochester, New York, the elements have combined to produce a near perfect living laboratory situation for big business and the arts to lend each other a hand. During the Spring of 1972, Nazareth College, Rochester Institute of Technology, and Eastman Kodak Research Laboratories got together to solve some problems about makeup for films and television. The result was a two day seminar using films, slides, closed circuit television, and live demonstrations for students, community theatres, Kodak employees, and all who might be interested.

During the last few years, R.I.T. film students and Nazareth College theatre students have been working together informally—with Nazareth providing actors, scripts, workshop performances, and dramatic scenes for R.I.T. students to film. In the course of this work, Joe Baranowski, head of theatre arts at Nazareth College, and Richard Floberg, associate professor in the film making and TV department (headed up by Reid Ray) at Rochester Institute of Technology, began to see that it would be beneficial for their students to know more about the technical problems of makeup application.

Although the theatre arts department at Nazareth is only two years old, it now has 20 majors. Projecting into the future, Baranowski saw that their training should be expanded beyond straight stage makeup. Similarly, Floberg and the R.I.T. staff felt their students would probably be more sensitive film and TV makers and technicians if they had some understanding of the basic concepts of making up for cameras.

In the Rochester area the logical place to go with a project like this is direct to Kodak. Earl Kage, head of the Research Laboratories at Eastman Kodak, saw an opportunity to do some testing of makeup application, makeup colors on various kinds of films. The results he felt would be beneficial for Kodak's own staff film makers as well as for Kodak film stock users.

The Schools

The R.I.T. program in film and television concentrates on the technology of the crafts as they relate to areas of commercial, governmental, scientific, or educational work. Floberg says the R.I.T. programs are unique in two respects:
1. Their students enter programs with a pretty complete knowledge of photography. This saves an enormous amount of class time and lets them concentrate on what to do with the process rather than teaching the process itself.
2. They encourage film making in any basic area of interest —including dramatic or entertainment.

Nazareth College is a 1,200 student, liberal arts, Catholic institution with a new fine arts building and a budding and active theatre arts department, which has three full-time and one part time faculty. The new arts center is the focus for touring shows that play in the Rochester area. In recent years, the college has been concentrating on one subject for a year long arts festival. In 1971–72 it was German Culture; in 1972–73 they are turning to what Baranowski calls the "illegitimate theatre"—carnivals, vaudeville, and clowning.

68

To coordinate with Lee Baygan's makeup demonstration, slides were shown: cleaning face (1, 2); after foundation is sponged on, highlighting under eyes (3); highlight (4); application to cheekbone (5).

With eyelids highlighted, Lee Baygan shadows the eyesocket bone (6), uses translucent powder to set makeup (7). After removing excess he then applies eyeliner (8), mascara (9), and liner again over false lashes (10); lightly pencils in eyebrows (11), dusts with dry rouge (12), and brushes on lipstick (13) to produce the no-makeup makeup (14).

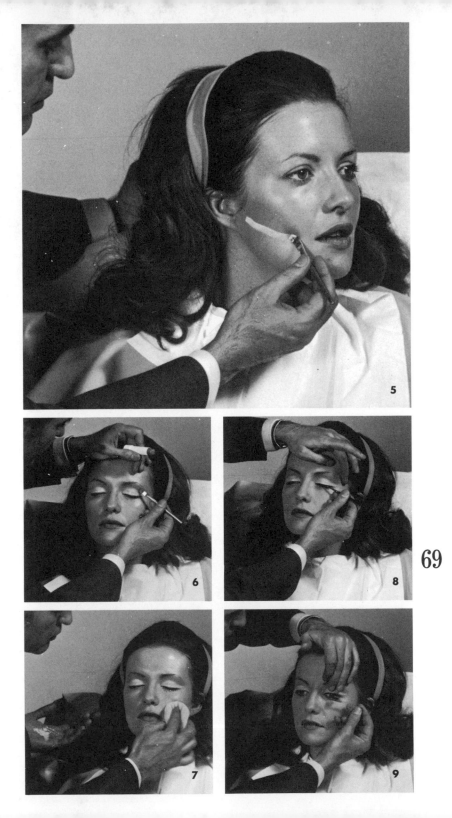

69

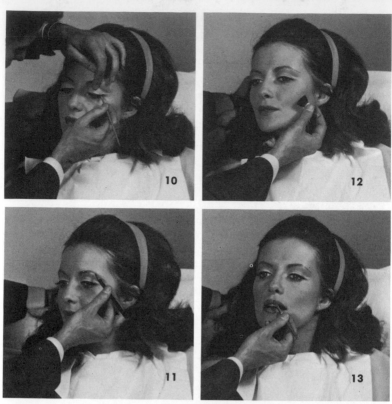

Setting up the Conference

Two well known makeup men were brought in to work on the project seminar. NBC TV's makeup department head Lee Baygan demonstrated methods of TV and film makeup application. Bob Kelly, theatre makeup and wig man, came to talk about his new makeup products and to demonstrate his theatre makeup techniques.

But, obviously, just doing live makeup demonstrations on stage was not going to teach much about how it will look at the different scales afforded by television and films. So, five or six weeks before the planned live seminar, Baygan and Kelly made a trip to Rochester to have their demonstrations filmed and photographed by Kodak. After the films were developed, they returned for the two-day live sessions, held at Nazareth College April 14–15.

The first day of the session consisted of Baygan demonstrating natural makeups for films and TV. Concurrent with this, color slides were projected to show in detail the work he was doing on the stage. 16mm films of the same demonstration showed how the makeup looked on actual film, under studio lighting conditions. A closed circuit television hookup, which originated from R.I.T., was used to show how makeup, film types, and lighting conditions looked on the TV monitor.

The second half of the day, Bob Kelly demonstrated his makeup techniques for the stage; films of his work were also shown. During the second day, seminar participants (including the technical people) practiced what they had learned on each other, under the supervision of Baygan and Kelly.

71

Kelly's work is not unfamiliar to theatre people. Because of the many theatre arts departments across the country expanding their vision into the areas of video tape recording and 16 mm film work, Lee Baygan's solutions for film and TV makeup are of immediate concern.

Changes in Television Makeup

Baygan began his session with a few remarks about the "old days" of television: "We used a lot more colors than now. The lighting was not as good. The cameras were not perfected. In black and white television we used to use a black lipstick and a yellowish or grey makeup. We used to do a lot of shading. By, that I mean, if people had wide jaws, or fat nose, or double chins, the first thing a makeup man did was to try to eliminate those prominent areas with a dark shade. There was a theory that everyone should have an oval face—no matter who they were, they came out of the makeup room with an oval face. Then came color television and we couldn't do that—or we would have created a monster. Putting dark colors on an actress' face wouldn't eliminate anything. We finally had to recognize that there was nothing wrong with a person's own face shape.

"Since the advent of color, we have changed our makeup about six or seven times because of the change in cameras," says Baygan. "Today, cameras and films are such that we have to use a minimum of makeup. What you see some people wearing in the street is 50 times more than we use on television. There we use practically nothing. When a model or actress leaves the makeup room and somebody asks 'Aren't you going to get made up?' That's the time I know I've done the best job for TV or films."

Makeup Manufacturers

Baygan stressed that most of the cosmetics that are sold for street wear are not right for television or film work, and went on to mention that at NBC studios they have a number of different makeups such as Max Factor and Stein's. Even though Max Factor is no longer making theatrical makeup, NBC had found with the manufacturer in California and the studio in New York it was difficult to maintain color consistency. Recently, Baygan has changed over to the relatively new line of cosmetics put out by Bob Kelly. For this seminar, Baygan and Kodak got together to select a number of basic products from Kelly's line which should go in a simple basic makeup kit for film or television work.

Colors for Color TV or Films

Makeup designer Lee Baygan considers that there are a number of other factors to consider besides how it looks to your eye when working with makeup for color TV or films. "There are lighting problems, costume and set design problems and when dealing in TV, video problems," Baygan points out, "and unfortunately in most TV studios all those departments work independently, and most of them are color blind." As an example of how this works Baygan mentions that the face which goes green or orange on your color TV set does so not because of the makeup but rather because something on the set or costuming is causing that color to bounce off the actors' face.

Nor does Baygan feel that the makeup artist can do anything to counteract that reflected color, because, as he points out, when that actor or actress moves into another scene, room, or costume with yet another dominant color, the face color will change again.

"The best advice I can give," continues Baygan, "about what color makeup to use for television and films is: the one that most closely matches the skin tone. You never go wrong—that's the best. If you have a trained eye for skin tone and watch most people closely they have a lot of green and yellow in their skin—sometimes a little too much pink. Presently the systems we have in TV and films pick up those colors so that something like a greenish or olive complexion has to be watched because without makeup those colors will all be transfered to the screen."

Step by Step Natural Makeup

The first step:—clean the face. Most women use anything from Crisco to expensive cold creams, Baygan uses a Bob Kelly product. He finds with the type of foundations he is using, it is not necessary to put any moisturizer on because there is a fair amount of oil in it already. "It has been the practice," Baygan comments, "to use a little moisturizer underneath, but it creates a lot of shine, as a result you have to powder it down, and when you powder it too much it becomes matte which cracks as soon as she smiles."

73

After cleaning the face, he then applies a basic foundation with cut foam rubber. "I can use natural sponge," says Baygan, "those are the two materials you can use but I use foam rubber because it soaks up most of the grease in the makeup, so what goes on the face is a very thin film of makeup. If the skin is blemishy and freckled, and you want a thicker makeup, the best application material is a natural sponge which you have to wet before applying. That way you get a thicker base that covers most blemishes. If the ears are exposed you cover them, if the hands come close to the face they should also be made up." Baygan then takes a clean side of the sponge, and wipes lightly across the foundation to make sure that the application is not too thick.

Highlights

Baygan usually highlights a face in two areas—on the cheekbones and under the eyes, if there is a discoloration of the skin. "The purpose of highlighting the cheekbone," he points out, "is to create a three dimensional face." "When trying to bring out bone structure I put highlight and then rouge on top of it in both the cheekbone and jaw bone areas so that the face won't be in one piece."

Eyeshadow

Many people in television use colored eyeshadow but because of the color reflection problem, at NBC they have eliminated all colored shadows. Now they use only two: a white and a brown. Baygan applies the brown tone in the upper area of the eye lid, along the eye socket bone, with the white below it. That combination of colors appears to the camera as a three dimensional curved eye, whereas if the white had gone on the bone areas, as is often done especially in fashion makeup, the lights and camera would make that bone too prominent.

Powder

74

At this point, basic colors have been applied to the face; Baygan powders this down to set it, before proceeding to mascara, eyeline, eyebrows, lipsticks and rouge. When using Bob Kelly's makeup, Baygan does not think one needs much powder. But in any event, he recommends a translucent powder which will not change the color of the makeup, and then uses a small brush to remove the excess.

Eyeliner

There are several different types: pencil, grease pencil, liquids. For his purposes Baygan finds that cake eyeliner is the best. He recommends starting the line at the extreme inside corner of the eye, following the lid line and ending at the lash line. He has found black too strong and prefers brown.

The Finishing Touches

Baygan applies mascara to the upper lash then goes on to use a surgical adhesive made by Johnson and Johnson to apply false eye lashes. He notes that the lashes should not be too long because an overhead light could cast unattractive shadows. For eyebrows he recommends a very sharp pencil and a feather-like stroke. "If your model has good skin tone, don't use rouge," he advises. The biggest problem is to place the rouge over the cheekbone highlight and then to shade it out. If you put too much on—its a mess to clean off. The final step is lipstick. The color has to be carefully selected not to be too red, too dark, or to have any blue in it.

Lee Baygan wound up his demonstration by commenting that unless the script calls for unusual makeup for men— one should use only just enough to cover skin tone and beard area.

Filming in Low Light

Commenting on these sessions, Earl Kage at Eastman Kodak Research Laboratories says that the best film they make for filming a theatre production is Eastman Ektachrome Commercial type 7252. But he points out that its slow speed of 25 usually prohibits use in the low light of theatre conditions. The best substitute is Eastman High Speed Ektachrome Type B, Type 7242. This is pre-striped, he said, so that sound can be recorded.

75

This type of two day investigation into the crafts of makeup and particularly for TV and film work would be a valuable addition to the curricula of the many schools where makeup is something students just pick up as they go along. The films used in conjunction with the seminar will be available through Nazareth College, and should constitute a very brief, but comprehensive basic course in film and TV makeup.

The status of makeup in our theatre today needs regular analysis and redefinition. Too much happened during the 1960s to assume that any of the crafts of theatre could remain the same. A whole New Theatre arose and developed in that decade. Television continued its march across the plains of culture. Perhaps more than any other of our supportive theatre crafts, makeup seems to have been reevaluated, repositioned in relation to its popularity, importance, and expendability during these developments. To approach it in the way it had been thought of since the 1920s would, therefore, be ostrich-like, and that behavior will not advance the art, unless the underground aspects of the analogy are doubly significant.

Actor Nicholas Kepros, who has taught makeup for five years in the Opera Theatre of the Juilliard School of Music, examines this new status of the craft. He justifies its continuation and continued study of it on the part of future actors; then he provides some practical pointers on teaching and studying makeup, which will delight professionals and intrigue students, as well as assisting them.

Nicholas Kepros began his New York acting career as a member of the Phoenix Repertory Company, playing everything from walk-ons to Hamlet. He spent several seasons in repertory companies across the country and also spent several seasons as

*guest artist at half a dozen universities.
His New York appearances have been in
"St. Joan" at Lincoln Center, in Robert
Lowell's "Endicott and the Red Cross" at
The American Place Theatre, "The Mil-
lionairess" Off-Broadway. He holds an
M. A. degree from the University of Utah
and is a graduate of London's Royal
Academy of Dramatic Art. During the
1966–67 season he studied in Paris on a
Fulbright grant and now performs fluently
in French as well as in English. More re-
cently he played the title role in the New
York Shakespeare Festival's production of
"Henry IV," and appeared as Basho in the
American premiere of Edward Bond's
"Narrow Road to the Deep North" at the
Charles Theatre in Boston.*

*The following article was first published
in "Theatre Crafts" in October, 1969.*

77

Understanding Makeup

by Nicholas Kepros

WITH the current upheaval in American theatre—an almost mania for striving after new forms and new modes of expression—the old techniques of makeup, diction, voice projection, and the ability to time an exit line seem suddenly to be of questionable usefulness. Do they even have a place in The New Theatre? Does an actor beginning his career as a member of, say, the La Mama troupe have any actual *need* for a knowledge of character makeup, for example? If makeup is ever used in that theatre, will it not most likely be in bold strokes for comic or grotesque effect? Finely-painted old-age makeups make strange bedfellows with strobe lights.

The demise of makeup on the professional stage is not a recent phenomenon, however. The art of makeup began its wane when American drama moved into realism. The ordinary folk of realistic drama, together with the professional theatre's penchant for type-casting, eliminated the need for transforming an actor. It gave the theatre a generation of actors whose knowledge of makeup reached its outer limits at a Max Factor pancake shade-number and a deft method for sharpening eyebrow pencils.

Now, theatre has once more swung out of the realistic, but not back to any drama we have known before—the

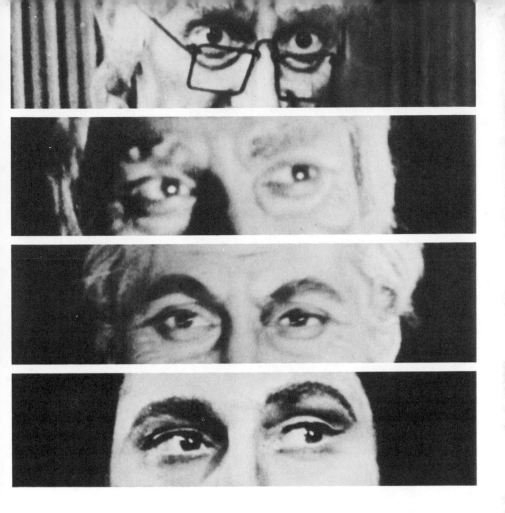

pendulum seems to have left the clock. In this theatre of
free form, which uses the actor's body as a plastic medium
—often nude, in the lap of the audience, and under vastly
varying light sources—what *use* is there for a technique
that delineates character and depends on distance and ho-
mogeneous lighting for a successful illusion? The answer
is, of course, none. However, in fairness, the question should
also include an examination of the possible longevity and
ultimate influence of this new theatre.

Whereas a limited perspective of our present theatrical
tastes would lead one to discard forever the knowledge of a
classical or traditional makeup (since even Euripides' Di-

onysus is now done "in '69"), a larger view sees the current *theatrical* trend as part of a *general* one which includes popular music, painting, and even education: this is the dawning of the Age of the Amateur.

On stage and on the school board, it once seemed to promise a breath of fresh air, but as time has gone by, the arrogant incompetence that was necessary for a release from stiff professionalism has begun to try the patience of the public. Each excursion to a garage or store-front performance leads to a rediscovery, by their absence, of the strengths of professionalism, not the least of which are dependability and a sense of structure. What we recognize is that this Age of the Amateur will not ultimately obliterate other forms of theatre, but will exist side by side with them. The salutary effects of the new theatre, such as the easy acceptance of nudity and the use of mixed media, will remain, and the professional theatre will be the lucky beneficiary.

Traditional techniques on the other hand will continue to be used, and taught, in those places not entirely tied to the exploration, or exploitation, of the latest fad. Where the word is still important to communication, the actor will concern himself with being heard; where audience involvement is understood correctly as a psychological phenomenon (and not a physical one, as with the naively literal Living Theatre), there will be an appreciation of its dependence on the *separation* of performer and spectator—on distance. And distance, in all senses of the word—physical, historical, and emotional—gives rise to the necessity for makeup.

80

Teaching Makeup

By far the best textbook on the subject is Richard Corson's *Stage Makeup* (Fourth Edition, 1967, Appleton-Century-Crofts, New York). Its encyclopedic range and unfailing good sense make it a necessity for every student of theatre. A less thorough (and less expensive) book is *Practical Stage Makeup*, by Philippe Perrottet (1967, Reinhold Book Corp., New York), still a good choice for the clarity of the text and the impact of the photographs, especially those of Sir Laurence Olivier.

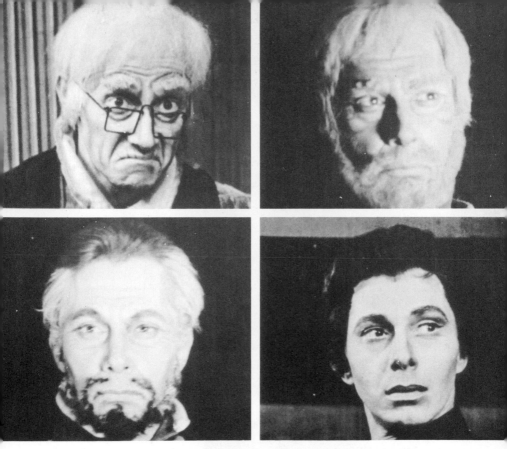

Actor Nicholas Kepros demonstrates a range from youth to age in makeup: Angelo in "Measure for Measure" (bottom right); Worcester's middle age in "Henry IV, Part I" (bottom left); the elderly Salisbury in "Richard II" (top right); and an aged Starveling in "A Midsummer Night's Dream" (top left).

Although there are some other usable textbooks on make-up, the techniques can only really be learned by an empirical approach where guidance, trial and error, and experience play important roles. Lack of guidance leads to gross misunderstanding of even the most basic techniques to be read in a book. A blackboard drawing constructed step-by-step with a commentary makes a much more lasting impression than a chart from a book; demonstration on the face of a student is ultimately the only really successful pedagogy.

In several years of teaching makeup, I have developed some approaches which might be useful as a supplement to whatever textbook a teacher may be using. Some of these

The same wig can be treated differently to create a character style for Malvolio in "Twelfth Night" (top) or for Marlowe in "She Stoops to Conquer" (bottom).

observations may seem obvious to those who have experience in teaching the subject; to others, they may prove helpful in a practical way.

The simplest medium for teaching makeup is grease paint in sticks. Once techniques have been mastered, it is easy to reproduce them in pancake, which is a relatively inflexible medium that takes corrections only with difficulty. The best brand of grease paint is Leichner (London) for texture, purity of ingredients, and faithfulness of the tones. An entire beginning course may be taught with base numbers 5 and 9, and four liners: black, white, dark brown, and lake. All fine work (eye lines, eyebrows, and lips) should be done with brushes in order to give maximum practice in their use. (Two flat sable brushes, Nos. 3 and 4, are sufficient.) A basic makeup kit for men would consist of the above together with some albolene and some transparent blending powder. Women would add a blue or green eyeshadow and some false eyelashes.

It is good to ask students, during the first session, what they consider to be the uses of makeup, and to guide them to a realization of the following three:

1) To project facial features across a distance imposed by the size of the auditorium.
2) To correct and beautify the features.
3) To change the features toward a particular character.

In connection with these last two, one should begin immediately to instill the habit of observing from life, whether it be simply the shape of an eyebrow or entire character types. Each student should also begin a scrapbook of photos to include all kinds of features—beautiful and grotesque.

83

A good method for introducing the principle of highlight and shadow is to place a white ball under a strong overhead light. Demonstrate that it is by the interplay of light and shadow over the surface of the ball that we perceive the object to be a sphere instead of a flat circle. Then take a pinkish ball and show that the color of the shadow is a function of the color of the ball, except that the *shade* is darker. From this it is a quick step to showing how an overhead light source plays over the curved surfaces of the face, and how the illusion of different proportions (more protruding or higher cheekbones, or projecting or receding chin) can be achieved through highlight and shadow. The ball may be placed near the cheekbone to show how similar the patterns of light are. A teacher can point out at this juncture that the color of the shadow here is again a function of the base color such as a pinkish base and reddish-brown shadow, or a yellowish base and brown shadow.

As a corollary, the light source can be shifted to footlight position to show the reverse effect on the curves of the face. A Degas portrait of a ballerina will fix this footlight-pattern in the mind of the student and strengthen, by contrast, his ability to imagine an overhead light source while sitting at the mirror. Today's teachers should indicate that this principle is dependent on the fact that the *actual* light source on stage is almost invariably overhead, and that the painted illusion would be destroyed in front of footlights.

The student will learn to blend from highlight to shadow only after several sessions, so it is best to clean up the messier attempts and move on to a consideration of the juvenile or straight makeup. I begin by teaching a straight makeup for classical plays, showing, after it has been mastered, how it can be modified and made more subtle for a modern play or a smaller house.

Following are a few pointers to supplement, and in some cases correct, most textbooks:

Eyes. 1) Black should be used for upper lash line (with black mascara) for all hair colors, men and women.

2) For line below eye: Brown liner for all hair colors. Black here tends to close the eye. This line should be more horizontal than indicated in most texts, not tilted up at outer angle of eye.

3) Show that placement and trim of false eyelashes can have widely varying effects.

4) Eye shadow is no longer placed on the eyelid but is to be considered as the shadow under the orbital bone (to be felt with the finger) which can be modified—imagined higher, lower, and longer. (Colors: brown for men; brown, blue, green, and others for women).

5) White liner gives best illusion when placed between eyeball and lower lashes.
6) The traditional red dot at the inner corner of the eye looks like a red dot at the inner corner of the eye: it should be abandoned at long last.
7) Give practice in blocking out eyebrows or parts of them (such as the under side for people with low brows) with soap or mustache wax before base is applied. Instill appreciation of the importance of shape, size, and placement of eyebrow to give impression of beauty, intelligence, stupidity, ferocity, and so forth.
8) Make a collection of successful eye makeups and encourage students to do the same.

Nose and chin. Show how highlight and shadow can lengthen, shorten, and vary the width of the nose, emphasizing the nostrils; also show how the chin line can be sharpened by this technique.

Actor Kepros's makeup for the character Julius Apolcalypse in James Paul Dey's "The Redemptor" (below).

Lips. 1) Men should be made aware that the masculine mouth does not take color on the lower lip, which remains very near the base color. Lip rouge for men should be thought of as *shadow* in connection with the overhead light source, which results in its placement on the upper lip and *under* the lower lip. (Refer to the way masculine lips are described in comic strips, which is basically this technique). Lip shape can be carried with spectacular success by this method.

2) Women may achieve startlingly real alterations by applying rouge to both lips as in street make-up, with the addition of a white outline, an eighth of an inch wide, above the upper lip, thus obliterating the outline of the entire actual mouth.

A middle-age makeup should be attempted next. Textbook illustrations and charts published by makeup houses are useful here, but blackboard diagrams and demonstrations on a student, with immediate imitation by the class, are ultimately the only sure learning process. Demonstrate feature-by-feature, with frequent trips by the student to his own makeup table, rather than a whole makeup at once. Students should work on only one half of the face, to save class time. When the entire makeup has been copied, doing the other half of the face becomes a review of the material at the end of the session.

When old-age makeup is attempted, a teacher ought to observe that, whereas middle-age is described in paint by light and shadow playing over folds of skin, old age is described by light and shadow playing over the skeleton, especially around the eyes and cheeks. Students should be encouraged to observe faces where there is strong overhead light and time for discreet study (as in subways and buses).

Several sessions should be devoted to various character types to give a feeling for caricature and period: dowager, flapper, farmer, tycoon, and so on.

A Restoration makeup should then be attempted, to show that a lighter base and finer features are required by the white wig. For this period women should attempt the "Dresden-doll look" afforded by a pinkish base, lavender

86

shading, and more noticeable rouge application. Then, depending on time and the inclination of the teacher, there should be work on racial makeups, unrealistic and stylized makeups, and exposure to prosthetic techniques such as nose putty and latex pieces, although the latter is really a subject in itself and requires some mastery.

Men should be taught to work with crêpe hair, since even those going on to become professional actors will find companies where another beard or mustache from the wigmaker "just isn't in the budget." This situation is more likely to occur at the beginning of a career, for as one progresses in the profession the wigmaker takes over; however, early experience in working with facial hair gives the actor a feeling for various "looks" and a knowledge of flattering (and unflattering) lines and styles, which will allow him to guide a wigmaker toward the desired effect for the character. In addition, costly mistakes can thus be avoided. Some tips for crêpe hair:

1) It is generally desirable to take out the *curl;* this can be done by ironing the unbraided strand with a steam iron. If no iron is available, stretching the hair against a hot light bulb or over steam will do the trick.

2) Liquid latex (Duo adhesive, made by Johnson & Johnson) is excellent for building a beard that must be used several times, although it will generally not last for more than six uses. (Spirit gum as a base allows only one use of the beard. It is excellent, however, for a very sparse beard or stubble). The latex is spread on the face over the area to be covered by hair. The strand of crêpe hair is then spread with the fingers to the desired density and the *evenly-trimmed* ends set into the latex, the desired length of hair snipped off, and the process repeated until all the area designated by the latex has been covered.

3) Practice will give greater facility in controlling thickness of the beard and in mixing hair colors (lighter on top, darker below; salt-and-pepper, and others) for a more realistic effect. A beard constructed in this fashion, since it approximates the manner in which real hair grows on the face, may be trimmed just like a real beard.

87

4) Beards built on latex should be fixed on, after the first use, with spirit gum, which holds more securely and does not build up thickness with each use.

Most students have a tendency to make up too subtly, since they are yet unable to appreciate the effect of distance and bright lights on the colors and strokes they are using. To counteract this, teachers ought to arrange to use the stage with stage lights from time to time. Makeups should be finished in the dressing room, framed by improvised bits of costumes such as hats and scarves, and viewed by students from different parts of the house. If possible, the effect of various light gels should be demonstrated. Also, if possible, show how a perfectly acceptable makeup under bright lights suddenly turns a fiery orange under night lighting, which has a strong violet component. Since an actor rarely has any say about lighting, his only recourse is to a makeup which sacrifices some ruddiness in daytime scenes so that it will avoid looking carrot-like in night scenes.

Actors should also be given some reassurance that a criticism of makeup is not a *personal* criticism. Too often critical remarks occasion withdrawal and despair, when a little re-thinking and retouching could save the situation.

The vastly subjective problem of "successful" makeup should be discussed. Whom should the actor believe? Very often the director is too busy (or too uninformed) to make more than cursory remarks about makeup, and there are even occasions when a director erroneously damns a makeup entirely, when a few judicious corrections are all that may be needed. Actors should try to assess the situation as dispassionately as possible and should enlist a sensible and trustworthy friend to report on the effectiveness of the makeup from various spots in the house. This procedure is intended only as a guide to controlling the noticeability of the makeup. *Style* is quite another matter, and is entirely the province of the director, who has the unity of the show to consider. One can influence the production, of course, by turning out a makeup that excites the director into suggesting that everybody move along those lines, but it is a good idea to remain flexible in this area and, when there are no specific notes on style, to be aware of what other actors in the production are doing.

A final point concerning the makeup course itself: how long should it be? It has been my experience that a two-hour session is the best length; if possible, a school should schedule two of these sessions a week for at least an entire school year. Universities usually schedule the makeup course for one term because of limitations imposed by the curriculum, but (assuming that the teacher assigned to the class feels he is prepared to teach a more extensive course) the point should be made that a one-term or one-semester course barely gives time to lay the base-work.

89

Some of the most imaginative, most highly professional, and most delightful work in makeup, masks, and wigs has been created for children's theatre productions. There, the primitive impulses and responses to theatre are still in their purest, most elemental forms. There, in children's theatre, also, a seemingly perfect balance of budgetary restriction and inventive pressure produces a combustion of designers' fancy; frequently that fancy blasts them off into the world of let's pretend or super-reality, that world of mythic fact and factual myth. This non-naturalism or surrealism provides a richness of analogy, simile, and metaphor that gives makeup, masks, and wigs for children's theatre a frequent if not inevitable sparkle. Adult theatre must often adopt this same child-like surrealism to reach similar peaks. In one way, designers of makeup, masks, and wigs for children's theatre produce a kind of pop art of their theatre crafts. They use common materials in uncommon ways. They take household objects, construction items, and packing materials out of context and use them to make up performers into unknown other-worldly characters. In the doing, their improvisation born out of financial necessity creates a new world of fantasy from our ordinary, commonplace, everyday items.

In a special issue on children's theatre, published in March/April 1971 by "Theatre

Crafts," managing editor Patricia J. Mac-Kay surveyed that much maligned theatre endeavor and arrived at some definitions, opinions, and recommendations. A precis of that overview is presented here, as it is in "The Theatre Crafts Book of Costume" so that both books can be autonomous and complete in themselves and not require reference to the other on the subject of children's theatre. That precis is combined here with the article on makeup from the same issue.

Patricia MacKay, a Smith College graduate, is managing editor of "Theatre Crafts" magazine, vice chairman of the committee on theatre architecture and a member of the board of directors of the U.S. Institute for Theatre Technology.

91

Making Faces for Kids

by Patricia J. MacKay

Children's theatre, for the most part, has been looked on in this country as a stepchild. In the minds of many theatre people, it conjures up visions of weekend and holiday shows, a house of noisy, restless kids, and an endless diet of sugarplum fairy tales and nursery rhymes staged by non-professionals who serve more as a babysitting service than any really theatrical experience. Children's theatre has been treated as a stepchild to be tolerated—but just barely.

In reality, children's theatre is much more important. To put it simply, without good children's theatre there is less hope of future audiences for live theatre.

Current children's theatre takes several forms. It can be theatre for adults with a broad enough appeal so that children are interested, like the annual Christmas run of "The Nutcracker," almost any other ballet, certain "adult" plays, or the circus that comes to town. Or it can be planned especially for children, as are puppet and marionette shows, and some television shows and films. Technically, the term

93

*Fables and realms of the
fantastic allow children's
theater scope for inventive
makeups, such as in the
Prince Street Players'
"Jack and the Beanstalk"
(top) and "The Emerald
Slippers" (bottom).*

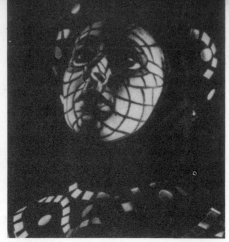

Makeup has risen to innovative and spectacular heights in the Orlin and Irene Corey productions for the Everyman Players. Irene Corey has designed mosiac faces to complement the costumes in "The Book of Job" (top, left and right; middle, left) and has adapted gothic sculpture into makeup for "The Romans by Saint Paul" (middle, right). For his part in "The Blue Planet," a Maximillion production, Ian Sullivan applies fanciful makeup.

The wicked Queen from Mill Run's production of "Snow White" (left) wears painted-on, super-scale, lower eyelashes.

Makeup is integrated with costume to create a statue-like Indian temple god (right) for the Children's Theatre International production of "Babu."

95

In "The Land of the Dragon" at the Playhouse in the Park, a full-face mask brings a dragon to life.

children's theatre is based on traditional theatre concepts— a play is presented for an audience of children—some companies include children among their actors, but most professional groups use only adult actors.

Few children's theatre groups across the country have permanent homes. And even groups with permanent homes will tour schools and communities. The very nature of children's theatre is such that touring is a way of life. In order to make money, professional groups must tour. Children's theatre, for the most part, cannot be considered commercially successful. There is money to be made, but not a great deal. Touring on a budget, then, is the single most important factor influencing all the technical crafts—most particularly settings.

Often settings are dictated by the transportation that the touring group can afford. However, because makeup, masks, and wigs (like costumes) are generally light and easily stored and toured, many children's theatre companies depend heavily on these design elements rather than scenery to convey the visual images of their stories.

Makeup in children's theatre does not essentially differ from adult theatre. While actual makeup materials, quantities, and supplies are virtually universal in all forms of theatre, application techniques obviously differ. Still, most professionals agree that having an audience of children does not influence their makeup styles. Says Jim Eiler of the New York City Prince Street Players, "Our approach is dictated strictly by the material, not by the fact that the audience is children."

However, the very play material for children's theatre usually contains a greater level of fantasy and the fantastic in every technical level than does adult theatre. Fairy tales, nursery rhymes, elaborate fantasies mean the three bears, the big bad wolf, Androcles' lion, witches, stove-pipe hatted villains, fairy godmothers—all of whom demand either imaginative makeups or masks. Often this fantasy gives designers of masks and wigs a freer rein than they would be able to exercise in adult theatre—wigs of yarn, wood shavings, or cotton organdy are much more readily acceptable in children's theatre than adult theatre.

The Blue Planet, a Maximillion production in New York City, uses exaggerated makeup, but in keeping with Peggy Simon's philosophy, the makeup is blue very simply because the story demands it. Similarly, in *Gabriel Ghost*, their villain wears a green mustache, not to be funny, but because references in the text actually state that the character wears a green moustache.

97

Perhaps the best known examples of makeup in children's theatre are the outstanding creations of the Everyman Players of Pinesville, Kentucky. Irene Corey has used makeup to create masks—a Byzantine mosaic makeup for Biblical characters in *The Book of Job;* for the *Romans by Saint Paul*, characters take on the faces of gothic statuary; and *Reynard the Fox* makes use of full-face animal makeup

One way of making animal faces is by the creative application of painted makeup-masks, as for a hare, tortoise, and dog (*top, left and right, and facing page, bottom*) from the Everyman Players' "The Tortoise and the Hare."

98

Animal fantasies, so common in children's theatre, allow a wide range of makeup designs. In some cases, an animal is created by the use of a full-face mask, as for Sparky in Maximillion's "The Fireman's Revue" (left), and a monkey from Children's Theatre International's "Babu" (facing page, bottom).

masks. Mrs. Corey has said, "I feel the all encompassing makeup mask is best (because) it frees the actor to become what he is playing."

While most professional children's theatre groups consider makeup an integral and coherent part of their productions, it is interesting to note that they are in a minority. A great number of groups take an exaggerated design tone and because their audience is children, they put on childish faces.

Peggy Simon of Maximillion Productions sums it up by saying, "I don't believe in 'clown' makeup for kids." Hopefully this visual playing down to the audience will disappear as more groups mature.

Wigs and beards are another design area for the uncommon use of common materials. The Paper Bay Players have made beards of crumpled paper (*facing page, top left*) and wigs of packing crate excelsior (*facing page, top right*) and floor mops (*facing page, middle*). In the National Theatre Company's "Androcles and the Lion," the lion (*left*) wears a painted nose and whiskers and a mane of knitting wool that makes an inexpensive and appropriately raggedy-ann lion for children. A maribu boa was used as a wig for CTI's "Baby" (*top left*), and The Paper Bag Players have made wigs of wood shavings and paper strips (*top right*).

101

As a detailed demonstration of teaching professionals to carry out makeup design diagrams and to apply their own makeup consistently throughout the run of a production, Joseph Cranzano's description of his makeup for Archibald MacLeish's "Scratch" is a paradigm. Transitory as the art of makeup may be, fleeting as a panned production may be, author Glenn M. Loney has captured the instant in Cranzano's design methodology, his procedures for simplifying and transmitting the essence of his designs into the craftsmanship of the actors involved, and his step-by-step application techniques. Following that description, makeup designer Cranzano also raises some accusing questions about the Makeup Artists & Hair Stylists Union and its effectiveness in theatre producers' understanding of coordinated makeup.

For a biographical sketch of Joseph Cranzano and for his credits, see page 43. Glenn M. Loney, a contributing editor of "Theatre Crafts" magazine, is a Professor of Theatre at Brooklyn College. He is also on the editorial board of "Players" and contributes regularly to "Cue," "After Dark," "Opera News," and "Dance Magazine." At present Prof. Loney is also at work on two books, "Opera as Theatre" and "Musical Comedy at Home and Abroad."

The following article was first published in "Theatre Crafts" in October 1971.

102

Joseph Cranzano's Ghostly Makeup for Scratch

by Glenn M. Loney

Archibald MacLeish's *Scratch,* which opened at the St. James Theatre late in the 1970–71 season, ran only three nights after Clive Barnes's review appeared in *The New York Times.* Since a negative notice in the *Times,* regardless of its validity, is as good as a death warrant for a new play, it was only common sense economics of producer Stuart Ostrow to post a Saturday closing so soon after the Thursday opening.

However, in the welter of phrases such as "this is the kind of play where nobody can win," Clive Barnes wrote: "I also much admired the ghostly makeups for the jury contrived by Joseph Cranzano."

To do him justice, Barnes rightly pointed out that, if his condemnation can close a show, his praise is no guarantee that a new production will stay open if the public doesn't like it. The difference in that comparison is, obviously, that the public, by accepting the Barnes Death Sentence the day after opening, had not even given itself the chance to find out whether the production had anything of value to offer.

Indeed, in relatively civilized lands, such as Britain, Denmark, Germany, and France, theatre audiences enjoy and savor critics' reviews, perhaps most when they are in

disagreement with each other, because of the stimulation such argument gives the intellect and the illumination of varied facets of play and production.

All of this preamble is by way of establishing that *Scratch,* both as play and as production, was hardly the disaster one might have assumed from reading the *New York Times.* If anything, the drama has viable stage values which will give it a long life in college, community, and regional theatre. It would not even be surprizing to find it,

For Archibald MacLeish's play "Scratch," Joseph Cranzano designed the makeup for a jury of the damned that was raised from hell to sit in judgment. The twelve jurors from hell sat in an old barn loft to witness the case between Daniel Webster and Jabez Stone, as they contend with old Scratch —the devil himself.

some five or ten years hence, being restaged in New York —but off Broadway, in an intimate playhouse; not in a proscenium house as vast and cavernous as the St. James— a theatre so firmly associated with musical comedies that many New Yorkers were of the mistaken opinion that *Scratch* would be a musical version of Stephen Vincent Benet's beloved short story from which it is adopted, *The Devil and Daniel Webster.*

The stunning settings by John Conklin filled the great St. James stage with a thoroughly realistic box set of a New England barn, with light seeping through the cracks of the rough, weathered boards, and the walls cluttered with an antique collector's treasure trove of old farm implements. Into this were dropped (from the flies) some charming and amazing 19th Century scenic devices for those moments not transacted at midnight in the barn of Jabez Stone. It is to this barn that the ghostly jury of the damned is summoned to pass judgment upon

105

Daniel Webster and Jabez Stone—the Whig politician who sold his soul to the devil—as they contend with Old Scratch, the devil himself.

Patricia Zipprodt's costuming was intriguing, and, as Barnes rightly praised, had, "a style and manner that goes beyond the strange pretensions of the play."

But, the most phantasmagoric visual elements of the production were the ghostly, ghoulish, mask-like faces that

Joseph Cranzano contrived for the jury and judge. It is seldom enough that *tours de force* of makeup are seen in modern theatre, so addicted have we become to the avoidance of "illusion" and its contrivances. And the so-called "realistic" theatre does not encourage much in the way of imaginative makeups, unless it is in the wizardry with which aging actresses re-create the bloom of long forgotten youth.

Maybe MacLeish was consciously trying to copy Shakespeare, in using theatre imagery to tell Old Scratch's story. Or, perhaps, the words just seemed excellent figures of speech. But, he does have Scratch tell Daniel Webster what the secret of his success is in winning men's souls from God:

"Men come to me as actors to the makeup table."

As it turns out, the actors who came to Joseph Cranzano did not have to barter away their souls for rewards in this world. They came to counterfeit the appearance of men who were already suffering their rewards in the next world for just such a bargain. How did Cranzano solve the problems of making up thirteen—Mr. Justice Hathorne presided—pitiable wrecks, vomited up from Hell, without making them look like carbon copies of each other? And, once the makeup masks had been devised, how was it possible to duplicate them night after night?

For *Scratch*, Cranzano had a crash program. That is, he had six days with the show in Boston to get the actors accustomed not only to the makeup devised for them—but also to applying it themselves. The process actually began well before the out-of-town tryout. Cranzano and the director, Peter Hunt (who also staged *1776*), conferred about the look that the twelve jurors and the judge should have. As Cranzano recalls: "Hunt did not want a horror makeup. No Draculas. He said. 'They should look like what they are supposed to be: men who have just been lifted out of their tombs. But not grotesque!'" Cranzano agreed with this because, as he notes, "If their makeups had been too unusual, too startling, they would have diverted attention from the verbal battle between Scratch and Daniel Webster."

107

The Design Concept

The first step for Cranzano was arriving at a general concept for the makeups. As he explains, "In most situations, I think the best makeup is to have people looking as if they're not made up. But this was a different case. Keeping Peter Hunt's image of men raised from the grave in mind, I decided on the basics of the makeup—the general colors, the method of application. I worked out various makeups on myself.

Faces of the individual jurors (page 106, below, and facing page) were based on a system of makeup that all the actors could apply themselves.

"There is a question about whether it is possible to create a makeup for another face, another bone structure," Cranzano continues. "But I never saw the actors until I went to Boston, and I couldn't wait until then to plan the makeup. However, certain general things could be decided, tried out. And then it was relatively easy to adapt them to the specific faces."

The basic colors Cranzano chose were yellow, white, and brown—with some black to be used around the eyes. "Yellow was the base color, with white for highlighting, and brown for shading," he explains. "Now, if I were doing my own makeup for parts like those of jurors, I'd probably use ten or twelve different colors. But most actors have little experience in doing complicated makeups. And I had only those few evenings to get them settled in applying the ghostly faces. So it had to be kept as simple as possible."

The Tryouts

After the preparation came the tryout. Cranzano's second major step was adapting his ideas on corpse makeup to live actors. To do this, he adjusted to such things as high cheekbones, deep set eyes, and thin faces, emphasizing and heightening such qualities to make the faces seem even more like those of men who had been long dead—though, of course, not quite decayed. "This was crucial," he says, "I had designed the makeups, but now I had to get the actors to relate them to themselves, in character. Actually, my concept was only a 'floor-plan,' if you want to call it that. Since the actors had to learn how to do the makeups, each man's own personality was bound to become involved—like seeing an actor's handwriting in his makeup.

"The difficulty was that there is such a volume of information to be given the individual actors. And even those who are old hands and have done their own makeups for years may not take in everything at one sitting. They can absorb it, follow you in the steps just so far, and then they may get lost. But each night is a little better; they remember more. As I worked on the makeups with each actor, I talked it through with him, step-by-step.

"And I stressed: 'Don't worry about making some mistakes. Even, if it's the sixth time you've put on the makeup!' By the sixth performance each man had his own quality in his makeup, but they were all related, harmonious. Nothing clashed in general color, style, or atmosphere. Each night I checked on the actors as they applied the makeups. And I helped them tighten them up, become familiar with the steps. Of course, some actors, a few very quickly got away from what I had devised without realizing they were doing so. In such a case, I always go back and re-do the makeup with the man, emphasizing the steps. 'Now, do it yourself! But do it exactly as I've shown you!' Well, I know it won't be exact; it can't be. I don't really expect that—but I want the actor to try. I found that maturer

The basic makeup diagram (left) was realized (middle) on actor Dino Laudicina (right).

actors had a feeling for making up that some of the less experienced lacked. That may not only be lack of experience, though; it could mean that younger actors are simply not taught much about making up.

"I never saw a group of performers work so hard and so well on makeup. They begged me for criticism; there were no false ego problems at all. On opening night, they were so good, we had only two or three minor notes on the makeup from Peter Hunt."

For purposes of simplification, only four colors were used: any black pancake, any white pancake, Stein mikado yellow, and Stein red brown. All were pancake to keep a matte, deadish look. The actual sequence of making up for *Scratch* involved the following steps:

1. Applying the yellow base over the entire face, neck, and mouth with a standard silk makeup sponge.

2. Stippling on the shadings, with the brown grease paint. Different texture sponges were used for this, to get a variety of rough, coarse facial textures: ordinary kitchen sponges cut into small pieces for the most mottled of complexions, and fine rubber sponges, but with wedged edges, to stipple in fine shadings around the nose and eyes, as indicated on the basic makeup diagram. The aim was to form a skull-like effect. By keeping this stippling coarse and loose, a deteriorated skin effect resulted.

3. Stippling black over eyes and under as indicated by dotted area on the makeup diagram. With a brush enlarging the nostrils as indicated.

111

Other jurors show the variety of cadaverous faces allowed by Joseph Cranzano's system.

4. Painting a white area under the eyes to effect sagging. Using a sponge to highlight the bone structure of the face with white to make faces look more sunken, sallow, ghostly, and skull-like, and to give the whole face a "crusty" look. For the latter, the application was quite arbitrary.

5. Painting all lines on forehead, around eyes, lips, naso-folds with a brush and red brown. The mouth was also out-lined, dropping one side lower to distort it. Nothing was blended; the coarser the look, the better.

6. Finally, applying eyebrows so that hair drops over the eyes, and applying wig.

"I didn't want any of these faces to look smooth. I didn't want the makeup blended. I don't even like that with *straight* makeups. That's why the sponges were so useful. We didn't use brushes at all. I wanted to avoid the danger of crisp, clean, clear lines in the faces. It worked much better to have them merely shaded, stippled. The black I used around the eyes, to make the sockets seem deeper, to add some definition here and there, to achieve a staring quality.

"It was important to have some uniformity of color and quality in these ghostly figures, as I've said—and, at the same time, individuality. But an interesting variation in the makeups is offered by that of Judge Hathorne. He was, as presiding judge, required to sit in an old carriage, in a very warm light. To make him look as though he had the same color values as the others who were lit by a colder light, I used more white with the yellow of the makeup.

"But even when you have designed the makeups it is difficult to know how effective they are until they are on stage. So I mingled with the Boston audience and asked people what they thought of the jury's makeup, and was pleasantly surprised that the results were good. In most situations, you don't want people to be aware that the actors are made up at all. They should look natural.

113

Who are you designing for?

"The question about theatrical makeup is what part of the house are you designing for? If you want it to look subtle to the first few rows, it probably won't carry much beyond. And if you want it to make an impact way up in the balcony, it will look too extreme in the orchestra. So I arbitrarily think in terms of the fifth row. The makeups will probably look a bit too bold, too strong closer than that. And, if they don't have very much effect in the last row of the balcony, well . . . who paid the most money for their seats?

"I'm reminded that Mike Nichols said to me when I worked for him on *The Apple Tree* and *Plaza Suite*, 'I want makeup for the critics.' There, the idea was to achieve maximum impact on the critics, more than anyone else. He had me work out Maureen Stapleton's makeups in *Plaza Suite* and after they were set, someone else came in and did them nightly. It was important that she look like three ladies of varying ages and types. Especially in the second scene, the one in which the big Hollywood producer is trying to impress his old high school flame—and it worked very well."

Usually, Cranzano says, actors are not the best judges of how they should be made up. Sometimes the problem is ego, but sometimes it's merely being unable to get any real or aesthetic distance from their own made up faces.

"I did Danny Kaye's makeup as Noah in *Two by Two*. He didn't see the need for my assistance; he'd been doing his own makeup for years. Which was true. What he did was a bland film makeup: fine for very bright lights and a camera lens working close to your face. But not good for a Broadway theatre at all. So I persuaded him to let me try out a makeup on him. I warned beforehand: 'You'll probably cringe when you see how it looks closeup in the makeup mirror. The lines will seem too heavy, too strong. But you have to remember that the audience is some distance away.' Fortunately, there was a full-length wardrobe mirror in the dressing room. I got him to stand on the opposite side of the room. With this greater distance between him and his reflection, he was impressed by the difference in the effect.

"You know," Cranzano continues, "what I'd really like to do during rehearsals sometime is to have a big wide mirror out in the orchestra so the actors can really see themselves as the audience in the fifth row does. You just cannot be objective when you see your made up face so closely and *only* close up.

Old Scratch—the devil himself (above)—says to Daniel Webster in MacLeish's play, "Men come to me as actors to the makeup table."

TV and Films

Cranzano has worked a lot in films and TV. Out of his experience there he has evolved some general rules, that echo those for the theatre. Obviously, when the lights are fiercely bright—often only from overhead, unlike much stage lighting—and when camera lenses are working close to the faces, makeups cannot be as strong as they need to be in the legitimate theatre. Still, Cranzano's basic concept remains the same: that the actors should not look made up. "I like to have the makeup 'stain' the skin—not plaster it. I quite agree that those performers whose faces look like a smooth mask of grease paint don't look natural. You really want to see the pores. On TV, for instance, if a man has a beard, I'll let some of it show through. But if an actor has very blond lashes, I may use a bit of liner. Or thicken an eyebrow, if it tends to get lost. And possibly a bit of rouge on an actor's lips—not lipstick—but just enough color so the lips don't wash out. Incidentally, some people think that suntans look just great on TV. They don't! A natural, healthy complexion looks much better."

"The eyes and the mouth are the most important in making up. If they don't work, you've lost half the face!" says Cranzano. He recalls working on George Segal, in *Loving*. Actor Segal was supposed to look a bit haggard, in his sagging forties. And he was game to try it—a contrast, Cranzano admits, to some performers who are over-protective of their image as glamorous, attractive stars. But this time, it was the film director who was dubious. Cranzano talked him into trying it out during preliminary screen tests, made in Segal's apartment. They agreed to shoot one take with the makeup and one without. When the director saw Segal made up, he said: "That's just the way I want him to look! But he doesn't look made up."

Films, however good they are for a makeup man's bank account, are hard work. On the set at 7:30 a.m. often until 7:30 p.m. with night shooting, on duty at 4 p.m. until 4 a.m. "It makes your life a jumble, especially if you have a family." As for TV, "you want to create, but you can't do much in TV anymore. Anything that *is* anything is coming from the West Coast now."

The Union

Oddly enough, though, it is with the film and TV industries that the Make-Up Artists and Hair Stylists Union has solid, standard agreements on fees and hours. There is no set agreement with the theatre. Cranzano believes that is partly because most producers are not even aware of how important makeup can be. They don't think it worth their while to hire a competent makeup artist to co-ordinate the show's faces, he feels. If the makeups are to be straight, they think each actor can do his own. That is not the case, Cranzano insists. Each one may very well be doing something different, however subtle. They may be working with different ranges and colors of makeup which do not make for a good visual effect on stage. "Not that everyone has the same skin tone, or degree of tan, of course," he continues, "but that there should be some kind of merging of general quality. If one actor is plastered with a ruddy mask of grease, another subtly made up, and a third bearing heavy liner marks like scars, the production risks looking grotesque rather than unified."

As a parting salute to the actors who worked so hard on *Scratch,* Cranzano says, *"They* deserve the credit in the *Times* review, not me!"

117

PATRICIA MacKAY

Circus makeup is in a different tradition from television's restricted naturalism. Those perennials of the patchwork harlequin variety are our all time favorites.

Now, however, we have lost contact with the basic distinctions between the various species of clowns makeups, and few of us can relate clown characters to clown actions. What the basic types are, how they are depicted, and how freely they can be reinterpreted are fundamental to an understanding of clown traditions. Two clown makeups are detailed step by step in the following article by Patricia J. McKay. It was first published in "Theatre Crafts" in September 1972.

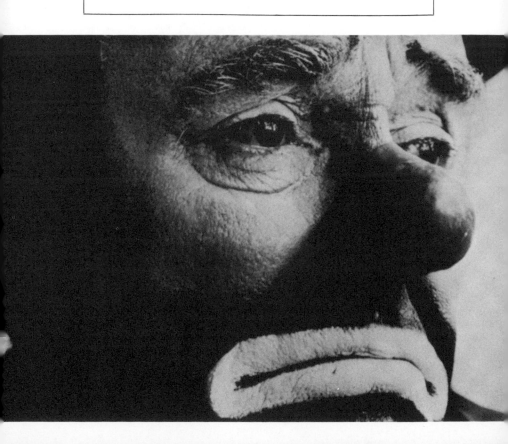

Circus Makeup
by Patricia J. MacKay

When the house lights dim, and the drum rolls, and the spots pick up the flying act doing a triple somersault in mid-air; or the high wire man vaulting over his partner who is riding a bicycle—the last thing an audience is looking at is the performer's face or makeup. Even in the big Spec numbers—the walkarounds, the Web, the cakewalk—faces and makeup play second fiddle to animals, elephants, llamas, horses, glittery spangled costumes or daredevil acts.

For the most part, makeup in the circus falls into two distinct categories: the general makeup worn by most performers—especially women; and second, the clown makeup.

The first type of performer makeup is a familiar exaggeration of standard street makeup. Whether it is the girl on the flying trapeze or the one under the elephant's foot, the makeup is standard stage makeup. Although in this context sequined eyelids and other outrageous makeups would be acceptable, the showgirls seldom have the time for such frivolities. Instead their makeup is the same kind and style worn by any member of a musical chorus, a dance group or a nightclub act.

The application is not "designed." Makeup is applied in such a way to accent and emphasize. It is more or less the natural reaction for anyone playing before an audience which sits at great distances. Particular use is made of lipstick, eye liners, and eye shadows to make the features of the feminine face carry.

119

Clown makeup on the other hand is quite unique to the circus. And, in this day and age, only strays into the "legitimate" theatre when a clown part has been written into a play, or, as in the case of *Godspell* or a recent *Romeo and Juliet* at the Folger Library in Washington, when a circus atmosphere is being put on stage.

Clown makeup, like clown costuming, is noticeably different from its counterparts in the theatre. In the circus, the clown character develops his own attributes rather than

Emmet Kelly's makeup reflects a tradition of clowns as Box Car Tramps.

fitting himself into a pre-existing and scripted part. Certainly, there is a long tradition in clowning, but each new clown develops his own character, his own act and routine, his own makeup, props, and costume.

From Village Idiot and Jester, to Harlequin, Pierrot, Joey, August and Today's Tramp.

It is generally agreed that today's circus clown is the scion of a long-lived house which has, at times, been dull-witted and dumb or clever and crafty. The medieval jester clown was often the dull-witted butt of any joke. Clowns as comedians and comic relief were familiar to Elizabethan England. In fact, one of Shakespeare's own troupe was a well-known clown. The *Commedia dell'arte* Arlecchino is perhaps the most directly theatrical ancestor of today's clown. He was transformed into "Harlequin" and appeared in England at the beginning of the 17th Century.

For modern clowning, perhaps one of the most important contributions was made by Joseph Grimaldi in the early 19th Century. His character now known as a "Joey" became the clown of the Harlequinade, in that particularly British form of entertainment—the Christmas Pantomime.

As Grimaldi played him, Joey had a wig with a single crest of red hair rather like the British Household Cavalry and costume which changed in character with his various roles. For example his big oversized pockets were for stolen food.

120 This character was taken into the "circus" that Philip Astley developed. Joey the clown was given a conical cap, was so loved by the crowds that he grew to be too-silk-and-spangle to participate in cake throwing or mock drownings. Auguste, wearing cast off clothing, became the new foil.

Clown Faces

Exactly how this is carried into the 20th Century circus ring is not easily unearthed. But it would seem that clown makeup (rather than costuming) is the repository of craft traditions. The makeup traditions of clowning seem seldom to have been committed to paper. Not even the Circus World Museum in Baraboo, Wisconsin (under most circumstances

a fund of information on any and all circus topics) could uncover makeup material. A somewhat strange fate for such a well loved theatrical genre. Circus histories seem singularly preoccupied with the glittery spectacle, and clown autobiographies are usually journals rather than investigations into their crafts.

What background there is, remains in the form of oral tradition and can only be gotten from the clowns themselves. Two of the younger clowns at Ringling Bros. and Barnum & Bailey's Blue Unit, "Sparky" (Don Washburn) and "Barnaby" (Bob Zraick), are well versed in the traditions of their craft.

Clown makeup is a highly structured art and falls into a number of divisions by type. First there is the Classic (pre-white face) Jester. Second, there are the white face makeups which divide into two distinct types: the Classic white which does not exaggerate any facial features and a Grotesque white face,

The "Barnaby" of Bob Zraick (above) is made up as a combination of an Auguste and a Box Car Tramp. The "Sparky" (below) of Don Washburn is in the tradition of "magical" clowns.

Changes in clown makeup, as well as costuming, between the 1910–20's (below) and the 1972 Ringling Bros. and Barnum & Bailey Blue Unit Clown Alley (above) continue to redefine deep traditions.

which perhaps has outlandish eyes, a large mouth or a huge nose. Opposed to the white faced clowns are the character clowns whose makeup is based on flesh tones. These are also divided into two further categories: the Rustic or Rube yokel type who does not necessarily exaggerate his features, and the Auguste which is a character makeup with extreme exaggeration of eyes, nose or mouth.

In addition to the Classic and Grotesque white face, the Rustic and Auguste there is another style—the only clown makeup to have its origins in the United States. It is the Box Car Tramp or the dirty necked clown. People see elements of the black minstrel in this makeup, but its genesis seems more closely allied with train-riding hoboes. As Barnaby explains, hoboes riding box cars just naturally acquire dirty necks and get sunburned, so makeup darkens their neck and upper part of the head. To get the cinders out of their eyes, the hoboes would wipe away a layer of black, thus leaving lighter tones around the eyes. Of course they grew a beard and they usually did a little drinking which made their noses red. After eating and wiping their mouths on their sleeves, this area too became lighter. The Box Car Tramp is also considered the offspring of the character Rustic makeup.

However, today, as both Barnaby and Sparky point out the differentiation between types of makeups have become blurred; there is no longer a distinct line which separates one type from another. Barnaby's own makeup is an example of how two styles can be used together.

Designing and Applying an Auguste-Box Car Tramp

123

Barnaby's tramp is Auguste because rather than using the natural eyes and nose of a Box Car Tramp, he has integrated exaggerated painted eyes and a ball nose into his look. Barnaby who was a commercial artist before he joined the circus also calls his face a "cartoon tramp."

In application, Barnaby uses Stein's clown white around the eyes and mouth first. Powders and dusts off. Then moves to the flesh tones; first applying Stein's #24 between the eyes, up to the hair line, and down the side of the face. He then uses a Stein #5 greasepaint on his cheeks and #18 (carmine red) to shade the flesh on the cheeks so they will appear rounder. After powdering a second time, he uses a

The rogue's gallery of clown
makeup shows white faces
and rustic designs as well
as combinations of the two.
The tattered Box Car Tramp
of the late Otto Griebling
(right, middle) is in the
tradition of the clown who
has donned a special witch's
costume for the Ringling
Bros. specs (facing page,
top left).

Wigs play an important part in the makeup of clowns, whether fuzzy and fanciful (above and above right) or bald pate (facing page, above left).

regular Max Factor makeup brush to apply the black outlines. Then blends black down his neck and shades a stubble beard. "You get to know your clown face pretty well," Barnaby quips, "and can practically do it in the dark. Hopefully, it looks precisely the same from day to day, but any variations are so minute that you are the only person who knows."

Sparky's White Face Grotesque

The makeup that Sparky has developed through his eight years of clowning can, he notes "probably be traced back to Shakespeare's Ariel—there has always been some type of magical clown." Sparky first applies clown white over his entire face. Powders down with a white talc until it is dry and fixed. He uses a Maybelline soft pencil to outline under his eyes and around his mouth before he fills in with color—black under the eyes and red around the mouth. Then powders these areas. The last (and tricky part) is the elaborate glitter eyebrows which Sparky applies on his forehead using unpowdered clown white greasepaint to hold the glitter, and by the same token, the glitter also sets the clown white, and keeps it from melting under the lights.

Noses

It may sound funny but clowns are complaining that "people just don't make clown noses like they use to." Some clowns find their noses in magic shops and gag and hobby shops. Often these are simply held on with elastic around the ears. Other clowns form red nose putty into little balls for their nose tips. But, as one girl clown pointed out, "it is very hard to wear a putty nose when you have a cold." Sparky does not always use a nose. His rigid vinyl nose is attached with a spirit gum to which he is allergic. He also will wear a rubber nose that can be glued on with Duo Surgical Adhesive.

Barnaby casts his own noses in latex—a technique that was taught in clown school by Hollywood makeup artist Vern Langden, the creative genius of the film *Planet of the Apes.*

The nose casting process is familiar to most theatre people. Cast a negative mold. Use modelling clay to build up the desired nose shapes on a positive nose mold. Cast that image. Scrape away the modelling clay and cast latex parts for the first and last negative mold. The resulting nose fits the clown's own and is easy to wear.

126

Barnaby comments that depending on your point of view Stein's latex is either too pure or too diluted for efficient clown nose casting. It takes too many coats to obtain a "workable" nose. Instead, Barnaby suggests that hobby store, pure liquid latex (often used to cast grapes or flowers) is the best material to use. Its consistency is rather like that of a runny whipped cream, and only requires 2 to 3 coats for a nose.

Wigs

A clown's hair is also important to his whole look. Some, like Barnaby, wear no wigs at all. Others have wigs especially designed to fit their image at Bob Kelly's or Zauder's. Still others find inexpensive wigs in retail shops that they can make work for them with a little bright colored dye. Many clowns, such as Ringling Bros. and Barnum & Bailey Blue Unit's "Tony" have discovered that the longest lasting wig is one that is made from a combination of human and Yak hair—a standard theatrical wig combination.

Putting it All Together

Like his makeup, the clown's costume has a long history. Sparky points out that the costume is a teeter-totter back and forth starting with the tatters of a village idiot, moving to the patched elegance of the *Commedia dell'arte* to the elaborate lozenge patches of the Harlequin and eventually back to the cast off clothing of the Box Car Tramp. In this country, as veteran clown Tony (Mark Anthony) reminisces the difficulties of touring with the beautifully white and starched Harlequin and Pierrot white costumes probably gave rise to the adoption by touring clowns (like Emmet Kelly and the late Otto Griebling) of patched, oversized tattered hobo outfits.

It is ironic to note that one of the public's overriding images of the clown is of "the broken hearted clown." The clown whose sadness and disappointment with "real" life made him chuck it all for the circus life of an itinerant jester. Strangely this image is, in part, true. Early clowns were physically unhappy. They were, in actual fact dying —being poisoned by the original lead-base clown white. Today however, there is no single clown image. The manifestations of each clowns' character is evidenced by his clothing, makeup, props, routine, and accessories. His face and costume are his trademark. And, while not an officially copyrighted trademark, it cannot be copied with success. For each face, its muscle structure and the makeup that works on it are as unique as the clown performance.

127

Oriental makeup with all its ritual tradi-tions and all its problems for Caucasian faces is so little used and so seldom required in the Occident that it is a novelty or special effect for most American makeup crafts-men. Whether the reopening of China to American exchange does or does not affect our general need to be proficient in the design or application of any kind of oriental makeup, "Theatre Crafts" could not pass up the opportunity to record the detailed work of faculty and students at the Uni-versity of Hawaii in the production of a Peking Opera, "Black Dragon Residence," which was originally developed by Daniel Yang at the University of Colorado.

Dr. Daniel S. P. Yang who directed the production and explained Peking Opera traditions, was born in Taiwan and studied at the University of Hawaii. He is on the faculty of the University of Colorado and was on a visiting professorship at the Uni-versity of Hawaii at the time of the produc-tion described in the following article.

128

Patricia J. MacKay who reviewed the production at the John F. Kennedy Center in Washington, D.C. wrote this article for "Theatre Crafts" November/December 1972 issue.

Makeup for Peking Opera

by Patricia J. MacKay

Ping Pong diplomacy made the breech in the bamboo curtain that got the President to Peking. And, in an America agog with China curosity—a rash of literature, quilted comrade clothing, and bamboo accessories—it is hardly any wonder that Dr. Daniel S. P. Yang's Peking Opera production, *Black Dragon Residence*, from the University of Hawaii was a hit at the American College Theatre Festival last Spring. To the surprise of many who went expecting a strange and alien evening, this particular Peking Opera is as close to a familiar, light musical farce as East and West can come. Still, it is highly stylized, replete with rituals and conventions—not the least interesting of which are the makeup designs and other technical crafts.

Far from being a fadish, coat-tail-hanger-oner, *Black Dragon Residence* was first staged at the University of Colorado in Boulder in the Spring of 1970. Recommended for the American College Theatre Festival the following Spring, the production made it to the regionals, but did not get selected for Washington. An associate professor in the De-

129

partment of Communications and Theatre at the University of Colorado, Daniel Yang was invited to be a visiting professor in the Department of Drama and Theatre at the University of Hawaii, which like the Universities of Colorado, Kansas, Wisconsin, and Michigan State has a well known program in Asian Theatre. It was Hawaii's intention to re-stage and re-enter the *Black Dragon Residence* in the American College Theatre Festival; and this time it won the trip to Washington, and the day on stage at J. F. Kennedy Center.

While the first Colorado production was sung in lip-synchronization to recordings of the opera made by professional Chinese actors, Daniel Yang's cast at Hawaii attempted the singing in Chinese. These vocal efforts and the student cast's mastery of the stylized acting gestures—standing, sitting, walking, running, and sleeve movements—drew a continuing chorus of Chinese cheers from bus loads of amateur opera fans in the Kennedy Center audience.

In order to preserve the utmost authenticity many costumes, musical instruments, props, and accessories for *Black Dragon Residence* were purchased from Swan Theatrical Costume Company in Taipei, Taiwan. In Hawaii supplimentary costumes for the on-stage musicians were designed and built by Linda Letta. A stage setting was designed by Wang Chung-ho, a technical trainee from Taiwan.

The Peking Opera Stage: a Soft-sided Box

130

A stickler for doing the production traditionally and correctly, Director Yang explains that "traditionally the setting should be very simple—partly because Chinese companies often have to tour and do not put much emphasis on stage setting. But, we wanted to do the show with all the resources we had. The University of Hawaii setting combines the essential features of a palace theatre and a good 'tea-house' theatre of the 19th Century. It was also inspired by the setting with which the great Chinese actor Mei Lan-fang toured the United States in 1930." The University of Hawaii set is essentially a soft-sided box set with latticed side walls and a back drop of embroidered silk with two curtain doors. Several Chinese lanterns hang into this space from a pagoda-style proscenium frame. At each side of this archway are

Scenes from "Black Dragon Residence" produced by the University of Hawaii.

projection screens which carry slides of the arias in translation.

Traditions in Makeup

During the hectic hours before *Black Dragon Residence* took to the Eisenhower Theatre stage for its matinee performance, Professor Yang took time to explain the formal traditions in makeup, costuming, and subtleties of color symbolism. Detailed attention to traditional roles and looks is very much a part of both makeup materials and the patterns of application. "In a sense it is rather like the Western *commedia dell'arte* troupes—the traditional Chinese theatre uses stock characters. Each of these stock characters has its own specific makeup and costume patterns. The costumes in traditional Chinese theatre are "theatrical" ones—devoid of historical accuracy and realism. By that I mean, a princess wears a certain costume type no matter which period in history she belongs to.

"There are four main role divisions in the traditional Chinese theatre; the male (*sheng*), the female (*tan*), the painted face (*ching*), and the clown (*ch'ou*)," Daniel Yang explains, "Under each of these main categories there are sub-divisions according to age and character types. For instance, the "female" role can be divided into five categories:

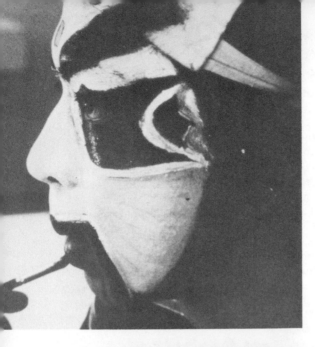

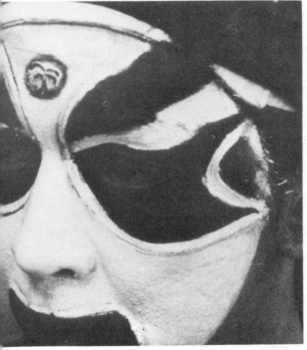

Using a scene paint and baby oil mixture and Stein's lining colors, bandit chieftain Ch'ao Kai applies his three-tile painted face makeup (this and facing page).

133

virtuous woman (*ch'ing-i*), coquette (*hua-tan*), female warrior (*wu-tan*), old woman (*lao-tan*), and comic female
(*ts'ai-tan*). Makeup for the first three categories is about
the same. (The full process is explained in relation to Valerie
Charles' makeup for the coquette, Yen Hsi-chiao, see photographs.) The old woman role wears no makeup, and the comic
female wears bizarre and exaggerated makeup—lots of white
powder and rouge, complete with beauty marks and so forth."

Elizabeth Wichmann, a student of Asian theatre who was
planning to spend the summer working with a troupe in
Taiwan, added, "The young scholar type of man would
have a face almost like that of the coquette, except that it
would have red streaks between the eyebrows that run upward to the hairline. The male clown has a plain face with
a white patch around the nose and eyes. It can go from the
middle of the forehead, over the eyes, and around under
the nose. Usually, it is white with some black designs in it."

Character Types

There is no doubt that the most spectacular aspect of the
Peking Opera makeup is the painted face—in *Black Dragon
Residence* there are two painted faces: one worn by Tony
Mebesa as the bandit chieftain Ch'ao Kai, and the other
by his emissary, Liu T'ang played by William "Young"
Saylor. Painted faces are generally reserved for men of
militant nature, and for supernatural beings. Both the designs and colors are traditional. The designs can be symmetrical or unbalanced. "When face designs get really busy,"
Elizabeth Wichmann points out, "and the design is crooked,
it is usually a bad guy. If a face is not symmetrical you have
a bad man with a tilted character. In this show, the faces
and colors are easy. For example, there is the face of the
bandit chieftain. Ch'ao Kai. His is called a "three-tiled"
face because there are three areas of one color separated
by three areas of another color. Those are placed one around
each eye, and one from the base of the nose to the neck.
The three-tiled face signifies an upright honorable man of
high station. The yellow base color of the patches in Ch'ao
Kai's face signify concealed thoughts—a person with something up his sleeve, scheming, and benevolently crafty. A
born leader type. The black and white in his face are used
as complementary colors. Liu T'ang, the Red Headed Devil

134

Makeup symbolizes the character-type coquette, such as Yen Hsi-Chiao (above) in "Black Dragon Residence."

—called so because he has some red hair and is as mean as the devil—has one of the more complicated makeups. It is mostly red and black with some green, gray and white. The black stands for loyalty and bravery. The red is essentially the same, but also suggests hot bloodedness. He is not too bright, but forever loyal to one person or one idea—the Little John type of character."

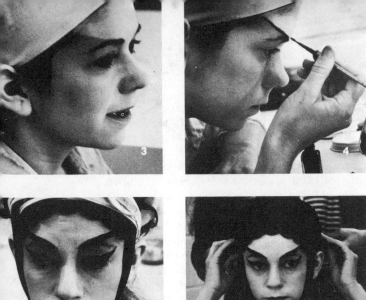

Application of traditional makeup and hair pieces, for the coquette role required two hours of student actress Valerie Charles' pre-performance time (1): first, she ties on a white hair wrap, and applies Max Factor white pancake using a natural sponge (2); then using Max Factor clear red No. 1 and shading with Stein's dry rouge No. 16, draws a diagonal line from the apex of the eyebrow to the hair line, and continues the line from the inside edge of the eyebrow down along the nose edge (3); with Maybelline liquid black eyeliner she draws on thick diagonal eyebrows (4), lines eyes and turns up eye corners (5); after applying false eyelashes and lipstick, she secures the first group of solution-soaked hair curls with twill tape (6); the remaining curls (seven in all) and long side pieces are wrapped to dry in place (7). The coquette's coiffure, called "great hair," is characterized, as student Linda Letter points out, by a loose tail of hair, actually a thread-like fringe that is 4 feet long and extends from ear to ear across the back of the head. A fake hair switch formed into a bun, and a black gauze covering are also added to the hair-do (8) before jewels and rhinestones are applied in a traditional order (9, 10) working from the center forehead curling around the head (11). Finally, flowers are added (12, 13); the hands and forearms are whitened, and palms rouged and fingernails polished.

137

Oriental Makeup with American Materials

The painted face is supposed to be shiney—the traditional makeup material is a powder mixed with oil. Holly Lindley, a University of Hawaii acting student who took on responsibility for the makeup problems of this show, came up with an American substitute for the unavailable traditional materials—baby oil and scene paint without a binder. "You just mix scene paint pigment with the oil in the palm of your hand until you can get the lumps out and it is spreadable," says Holly Lindley talking about her find, "it was a risk because the scene paint contains raw chemicals and we had to patch test for allergies on the actors. The red, black, yellow, and gray colors in the painted faces are the scene paint-baby oil mixture. The green, white, and any other colors are Stein's lining colors."

Dr. Yang commenting on the adaptation in makeup material notes, "in the production we tried to use American makeup where we could—it produced just about the same results. Traditionally, the white base on the face of Yen Hsi ch'iao, the coquette, should be rice powder mixed with sugar and water. After steaming, that mixture produces a cake. You cannot use clown white as a substitute, it is too sticky. So we are using Max Factor white. It does not give as heavy a white a base as the Chinese mixture would, but it looks fine under lights and from a distance. The scene paint and baby oil mixture produces as intense a color as the traditional Chinese pigment." Yang goes on to speculate that the Chinese are still using traditional makeup because it is cheaper, "but the American makeup probably works better if you could get it in China."

138

They all agree that there is no really effective substitute for the wood shaving solution that is used to stiffen real hair pieces for the coquette's coiffure. While it is possible to use egg whites, instead, the result is not the same. Hot water is added to the special wood shavings (from the *Machilus Pauhoi Kaneh* tree) and left to soak over night. When squeezed they produce a sticky juice into which the hair pieces are dipped, then combed and shaped. As they dry, they retain a desired shape.

Oriental Makeup and the Caucasian Face

An interesting problem arises in adapting painted face patterns from the broader Chinese face to the narrower

Bandit Chieftain Ch'ao Kai (played by Tony Mabesa)
wears the spectacular makeup of a traditional
painted face role.

Caucasian face. The answer is usually trial and error experimentation to get the right proportions.

The eyes are a special problem, as might be expected. For the University of Colorado production, Director Yang had his cast using tapes attached with spirit gum which then were pulled back and anchored, to create a slanting look to eyes. By the time his Hawaii crew reached Washington, this method had been discarded and the diagonal lines of the makeup were relied upon to carry the effect.

When the makeup is complete the actor's head is wrapped. In the Chinese theatre, the wrap is usually gauze. But, as Holly Lindley points out, "here in *Black Dragon Residence,* we have to use black cotton. It cannot be sloppy—leaving whisps of blond or brown hair. The wrap gives the illusion of a Chinese bowl hair cut and delineates the line of the face, acting as a frame—on the practical side, the wrap is used as a base to pin hats to."

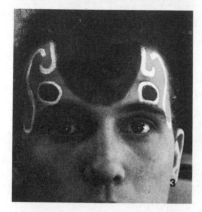

To create the painted-
face makeup for Liu
T'ang, the Red Headed
devil, William "Young"
Saylor (1) first cleans
his face with alcohol,
then covers it with
Pancro No. 24 to make
the scene paint and baby
oil mixture easier to
spread. Rather than ap-
plying his makeup in the
traditional order, he
does what is easiest for
him (2–6).

The Beards

A finishing touch in the complete makeup and costuming of many male characters in the *Black Dragon Residence* is a beard—but one quite unlike any standard Western wig. Long strands of hair are knotted onto a wire that hooks behind the ears and runs across the face above the upper lip, covering the mouth. Daniel Yang says, "I can think of three reasons for the beard covering the mouth. First, with the beard hung around the ears it *has* to rest on the upper lip. Then, having the mouth wide open for extended singing is not pleasant to look at, so the Chinese actors simply cover the mouth with the beard. And finally, there is a technique by which an actor blows his beard to express anger—without the beard over the mouth, the technique would be lost.

Green, red, white, and black are the dominant colors of the final Liu T'ang face (7).

141

"Three types of beards are used in *Black Dragon Residence*" Professor Yang continues, "Ch'ao Kai, the bandit chief uses a full beard which covers his entire mouth and chin. It is of exaggerated length—typical for the painted face characters. Liu T'ang, the Red Headed Devil, also has a full beard, but the mouth portion is open so that his lips are revealed. This type of beard is for a tough character who does not have a high station. Liu's beard is black, but there is a streak of red in it—suggesting that he has a red mole by his upper lip which produces red hair. The beards worn by Wu Yung, the Chief Councillor and Sung Chiang, the court scribe, are the "three-stranded" type. This is divided into three portions—one by each ear and one in the middle. This kind of beard is worn by middle aged men of civil nature—like scholars and civil officials."

Color Traditions

One of the most fascinating aspects of makeup and costuming is the use of colors to signify types, moods, or personality traits. "Chinese theatre started around the 13th Century," Daniel Yang continues, "over the last seven centuries, a rigid system of color symbolism in makeup and costume has developed. For instance, a yellow ceremonial robe (technically called the *mang*) is reserved for none but an emperor. But, in *Black Dragon Residence*, the bandit chieftain is nick-named "Pagoda-Lifting Heavenly King" so he wears a formal robe in yellow with dragon designs—the same as a king would wear. In the West, purple is usually worn by people of high position; in the Chinese theatre many shades of purple are worn by older people. Black suggests poverty and non-existance and is worn by ghosts and poor people. A beggar wears black with colored patches to suggest tatters. In the West, white suggests purity; in China it suggests mourning. The widow wears white and during a funeral scene all the stage properties are covered in white. Red is for all happy occasions; the bride wears red, with a red scarf covering her face. A scene of festivity is often marked by the lavish use of red decor—carpets, pillars, table cloths, chair covers, candle sticks, and candles."

The whole production is introduced by a gray-garbed stage manager, who explains the customs and traditions of the Peking Opera for the uninitiated. With wry humor he

142

points out that while this simple room contains only one table and two chairs, the actors will pantomime the room into a house, a city street, or a mountain path—whatever is called for in the script. The suspension of disbelief required of a Peking Opera audience is far greater than in the West: two chairs can become a mountain lookout, or a well to throw oneself into; actors open non-existent windows and are struck by the morning sun, and step stylishly over invisible doorsills.

While a Chinese audience would seldom be lost amid the familiar stylized symbolic gestures, they are also helped along by the fact that most Peking Opera tales are as familiar to them as Robin Hood and Tom Sawyer are to American audiences. The roles are traditional. The characters are entirely familiar and certain costumes and face makeups have become so inextricably bound up with their image that a Peking Opera devotee could look up from his table in the teahouse theatre and immediately recognize the character and role by the costume and makeup.

In every step and each detail the Peking Opera is conscious of tradition. How it was done; how it always has been done. The Peking Opera constantly reminds its audience that this is theatre—not life—it is presentational rather than representational. The complete antithesis of contemporary experimental Western Theatre, the Peking Opera is an ordered predictable ritual, one which the cast from the University of Hawaii under the direction of Dr. Daniel S. P. Yang recreated with an unusual combination of fun and scholarly style.

143

144

No book on the current designers, materials, and crafts involved with makeup, masks, and wigs can be complete without acknowledging the special contribution of Richard Corson. Quiet and modest as he may be in person, the vigor and volume of his work have been an influence throughout the field for over thirty years. In three published works his analysis of the historical background and current status of three distinct areas of the field—makeup, hair styles, and eyeglasses—has been encyclopedic. It has given theatre craftsmen a new scale of vision and endeavor—a broader scale which comprehensive overview thrusts us into. Whatever makeup designers knew before is corroborated, amplified, and given historical perspective in Richard Corson's essential publications; the impetus of our own personal invention can be backed up by his immediately accessible research.

Jody Brockway, who outlines the career and approach of Richard Corson, is a free lance writer specializing in theatre and film. She received her B.A. in English literature from Boston University and has contributed to "After Dark" as well as to "Theatre Crafts."

The following article was first published in "Theatre Crafts" in January/February, 1973.

The Face Painting and Furnishing of Richard Corson

by Jody Brockway

In the magic-making, paint-pots-and-powder world of theatre, the considerable contributions of author, teacher, and makeup consultant Richard Corson are widely known to both professional and school-level people. His consummate knowledge and technical expertise in makeup result in his continually being called in for makeup consultations by actors and designers. His extraordinary, voluminous book, *Fashions in Hair* is considered invaluable by professional hair stylists, whether working on Broadway, in television, or in film. According to theatre hair and wig designer Bob Kelly, "no school should be without it." Most college and university libraries contain author Corson's *Stage Makeup*, which librarians at Lincoln Center's Performing Arts Library consider to be "unquestionably the best book on the subject." Richard Corson has written the basic book on makeup, the definitive survey on hairstyles, and, most recently, on eyeglasses.

His interest in theatre—and theatre makeup in particular —dates back to childhood. In high school he sufficiently impressed dramatics teachers to be allowed to create all the makeup for school plays. From high school in Illinois, he went on to get a BA in speech and theatre at DePauw University, and an MA in theatre at Louisiana State University.

While at LSU, his early working experience was as Technical Director of the Workshop Theatre; then he became Technical Director at the University Theatre, Women's College of the University of North Carolina, and, later, Technical Director of the Experimental Theatre at Vassar. He also taught stage makeup at both LSU and North Carolina. Currently he travels around the country teaching one- and two-week workshops in makeup at various educational institutions.

As early as his college years, Richard Corson began developing theories on makeup, and wrote the first edition of *Stage Makeup* while teaching at LSU. That was 1942 and there have been 4 editions since. A major book, it's publication brought new thinking to the subject.

"When I first wrote *Stage Makeup* I related makeup to art—drawing and painting. That was really the first time that had been done, and of course it makes all the difference in the world. Before that, people had been told to put a brown line here and a white line next to it and that was a wrinkle. Of course it wasn't, it never will be, but that's what they used for wrinkles."

"It took me a long time to work out my theories on makeup. Now that I look back it shouldn't have; it all seems so obvious. You use the same principles that an artist uses in paintings. You look at those and do the same things, essentially, on the face."

146

It is these artistic principles underlying makeup, rather than techniques, that Mr. Corson teaches his students. Too often, he feels, students are taught to "do this or do that" to achieve the correct makeup. What they end up with is a realistic looking makeup job, not a realistic looking person. The principles he stresses are light and shade, color and character analysis; each principle relates to the next and must be comprehended within that interrelationship. His students begin studying light and shade by doing sketches in charcoal and chalk on grey paper—grey representing the flesh tones of the face. In this way they become familiar with making an object three dimensional on paper before tackling the face.

Then they go on to color, first color in general—which primary colors should be used to achieve which secondary colors —then selection of color for a particular makeup. When it comes to selecting colors for the final makeup, Corson puts a great deal of emphasis on character analysis in an effort to avoid "types." He feels there is no such thing as "middle-aged makeup" or "old age makeup," despite the existence of pan sticks from certain manufacturers called "Old Age Sallow." He opposes this "typing" of makeup because all old people are not automatically sallow and because young people also can be sallow.

Consequently, he explains to students that the characters they are making up are people, and asks them before they begin the makeup, to consider factors such as the environment of the characters, the racial strains that might be present, the profession, the kind of life they live, their temperament—age is only one of the factors. Only on the basis of such an analyis should a makeup artist decide what color base to use, and what color shadows would be appropriate for the chosen base.

Once the colors have been applied, the next question to be asked is what effect light will have on the pigment colors. Richard Corson instructs his students to determine where the light is coming from, where the light is going to hit, and what will happen when the light hits. To help students learn what happens when a colored light strikes the object, they hold different gels over a spotlight, and see, for example, that if there is a lot of blue for moonlight, they have to be careful of their rouge or it will turn black.

147

"Students should also think about projection—is it a big theatre or a theatre in the round? You must project certain features, but there is a misconception some people have that in a big theatre you can get away with anything—that you can just make everything very broad. But that will look false. I believe that if you do makeup convincingly, realistically, it will be convincing to the people in the first row and if the people in the last row can see you at all, it will be convincing to them. There are of course, certain features which should be emphasized, such as the eyes. And also, it is better to emphasize larger areas of the face that will project rather

than paying so much attention to small details. Too many people fuss over making a lot of tiny wrinkles. They are hard to do in the first place—to make them really three dimensional—and if you do make them very carefully and they look good close up, from the back they can't be seen; they just blend in. So I suggest you begin by projecting the large fleshy areas and the bone structure—that is what the audience will see. By highlighting these areas they will project to the back rows because light reflects from the highlights not the shadows. Shadows absorb the light.

"I put great emphasis on highlights rather than shadows.

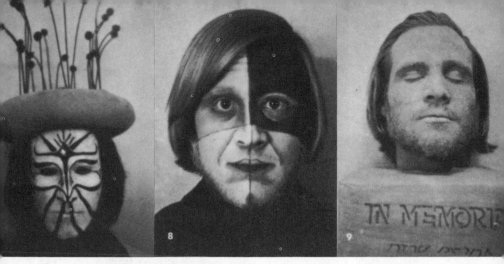

Richard Corson demonstrates his
makeup techniques by transforming
his own face into painters Vincenzo
Gemito (1) Giovanni Mannozzi da
San Giovanni (2), Jean-August
Dominique Ingres (3), and Bruce
Crane (4). He also makes himself up
as a crusty old man (5). Doug Massey,
a Corson student, has executed
makeups of a troll with deep pocketed
eyes (6), a feline-looking makeup-
mask (7), a quartered commedia dell'
arte face mask (8), and a tombstone-
like death mask (9).

I have students begin with highlights and do an entire
makeup with nothing but highlights, because it makes sense
to begin with what the audience will see, not with what they
won't see. Then they look at how much has been accomplished
with the highlight. The base, if it is reasonably dark, becomes the shadows. If additional shadows are needed, then
they can put them in. Normally they would put the shadows
on first and the result quite often looks like dirty spots. Plus
it's much easier to bring down the highlights if they are too
strong, than it is to lessen the shadows.

149

"You can start with white and stipple it down. Stippling
is very important and it isn't used enough. Stippling means
taking a sponge, putting paint on it, and touching up over
the base so that it makes a pattern of the sponge holes all
over the face. This gives texture. It's especially important
for young peoples, college students who are playing an older
part. No matter how much modeling you do, their skin is

Mid-1st Century A.D.

1780. French.
Marie Antoinette

French. Opera glass.

1850

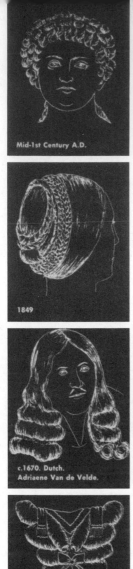
1849

c.475 B.C.

c.20 B.C.

c.1778. French.
à la Driade

Chinese eyeglasses
with weighted cords

c.1670. Dutch.
Adriaene Van de Velde.

1776. Italian. Lady's maid.

Greek. 6th Century B

c.1780

Early 2nd Century.

Probably c.140 A.D.

Italian. Bibbiena
(Francesco Galli),

1682. German

1674. Italian Painter

Chinese eyeglasses.

Fifth Century B.C.
Zeus.

1682. German

1774. French

44

French. Prospect glass.

48

c. 1650. French

eek. 6th Century B.C.,
hlete

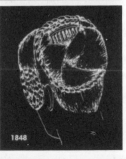
Fifth Century B.C.

Selected hairstyles, eye-glasses, and eye pieces (left) from Richard Corson's "Fashions in Hair" and "Fashions in Eye-glasses" show the crossing of styles over the centuries.

151

e 1st Century A.D.

1848

smooth underneath; so stippling is the best way to take away the smoothness. Usually I stipple with at least three colors.

"In teaching principles, my intention is to make myself expendable. So that when I'm gone the students are able to use these principles for whatever comes up rather than have to ask how to do something. I try to get them to criticize themselves, ask themselves what they intended to do, and whether they achieved it, if not, why not?"

Why does he think that the trend in makeup today is toward realism, naturalism?

"Because acting is more realistic now, therefore makeup is. The old method of stage makeup was intended to be real also, I'm sure; at a distance they convinced themselves that it looked real. Of course it didn't. On the other hand, realism can go to extremes, such as in Peter Brook's *Midsummer Night's Dream* a few seasons back where most of the actors literally wore no makeup and looked terrible. That didn't contribute anything. It merely called attention to itself, people kept looking at them thinking why do they look so terrible?"

Richard Corson is now at work updating *Stage Makeup* for the Fifth Edition, due next year. He is adding new materials, new makeup materials, that have come out since the last edition, many new photographs and illustrations which he has been collecting since 1967, and of course, new ideas.

History of Hairstyles

Hair styles and makeup obviously go hand in hand. As a makeup artist and teacher Mr. Corson frequently became involved in advising on hairstyles and wigs for period plays. Discovering the lack of detailed information available on hair fashions of years past, he became especially curious about the history of hair. As a result, a second book of his appeared in 1965, titled *Fashions in Hair: The First 5000 Years.*

A most unusual book, it is really the only one of its kind. Culled from representative paintings, sculpture, literature, and artifacts of the periods (including two rare books written by hairdressers in the 18th Century), many variations in hairstyle are shown for each period, in a total of 3500 drawings, period engravings, and caricatures. The hairstyles duplicate the actual modes worn by people on the streets, not by actors on the theatrical stages. And with comprehensive coverage of both men's and women's styles, as well as men's moustaches, beards, pigtails and wigs, the book does not restrict a designer to a few choices.

Factual information identifies the style by year and nationality, which after the ancient civilizations, are primarily English, French, or American; within the Western world, England and France predominate because London and Paris were the trend setters in fashion and were therefore copied by the other countries. In some cases they are identified by social class or occasion, such as "hairdo for the Opera." Instructions are given on how to construct the more elaborate and intricate styles, and recipes are supplied for hair preparations, ointments, pomades, dyes, and powders. A hair stylist faced with the task of creating wigs or fixing an actor's own hair in the fashion of 15th Century England, or late 19th Century France, need only refer to the appropriate section of the book to be inspired. Wig designer Bob Kelly uses *Fashions in Hair* as the bible catalogue of the field. He says "The book is invaluable to me: for example, when a school calls us to order wigs for a play, I always refer them to Corson's book. I tell them to give me the exact page and plate number of the hairstyle they have in mind; then I go to my copy, I see exactly what they want, and I make the wigs."

Beginning with the Ancient Egyptians, the material surveys Greeks, Romans, Anglo Saxons, and comes up through the centuries in Western Europe and America, ending in the mid 1960's. Mr Corson considered the Egyptians a practical starting point since little was known of hairstyles before that time.

153

"My original intention was to make this a book of illustration of hair styles to be used as a practical guide in producing historical plays," says author Corson. "I thought it would be a little book, a few plates and that would be it. Then I got started and the material began piling up. I felt that all the available material should be in one place so I just kept on going. It turned out to be 700 pages."

Researching the book, which he undertook at the suggestion of British publisher Peter Owen, he spent five years in museums, galleries, libraries, and rare book rooms in New York, Chicago, Rome, London, Florence, Amsterdam, Copenhagen, to name a few of the cities. The best, most lucrative collections he found were in the British Museum, the New

York Public Library, the Uffizi Gallery, Florence, and the Louvre in Paris.

After his exacting work in authenticating hair styles, how does Mr. Corson feel about the use of contemporary hair styles in period plays? We are all familiar with seeing Shakespeare or Greek tragedies performed in period costume with contemporary hairdos. Does he feel this can be done?

"No! Why should it be? I feel very strongly about that. That's something that has been done a lot, especially for men. If they're going to do period costumes, why shouldn't they use period hair styles? They can always use wigs, and they don't use wigs often enough, although now with men wearing their hair longer it's easier, you can do a lot more with their natural hair."

Spectacles, Eyeglasses, Lorgnettes

Finished with hair, the indefatigable Mr. Corson continued his research in yet another area—eyeglasses. "You very seldom see correct eyeglasses on stage or in film," the author notes "so I thought there was a need for a book." *Fashions in Eyeglasses*, published in 1967 fills that gap by tracing the history of eyeglasses through seven centuries beginning with their invention in the 13th Century.

"Early glasses were just different lenses sold by spectacle peddlars, and you looked through all the pairs until you found one that improved your vision. There was no such thing as individual prescription. And it was a long time before anybody in the Western world thought about anchoring them to the ears. In China, very early, they tied strings with little weights on them around their ears. But for the most part the glasses clamped to the bone in the nose and you simply held your head up. It was later than the 17th Century that somebody thought of extending a piece around the ear."

This intriguing and unusual source book supplies 500 detailed and annotated drawings and 120 period prints showing the manufacture, selling, and wearing of spectacles and other optical devices. Now costume designers have no excuse for having incorrect eyewear in their productions.

Theatre design has benefited enormously from the enlightened ideas and from the meticulous and unique scholarship of Richard Corson.

Down through the ages, men and women of all cultures and countries have worn masks in many other situations and activities than in theatre. However familiar their various forms in theatrical enterprises, face coverings from the other endeavors of life—from primitive masks to space helmets—have, doubtless, never been assembled and investigated from such wide sources and at such inclusive scope as in an exhibition called "Face Coverings," which was shown at the Museum of Contemporary Crafts in New York during 1970. The exhibition investigated, through a collection of objects and photographs, the many ways in which man transforms, disguises, protects, and enhances his face. It investigated his doing so for the purposes of religious ritual, festival, theatre, sports, occupational necessity, sexual attraction, and fashion. It investigated masks and makeup from Africa, the Orient, South America, and from American Indians as well as from contemporary artists with unusual approaches to the art of covering a face. While specifically theatrical applications were limited, the entire show was illuminating to theatre people. When the following illustrations from that exhibition were published by "Theatre Crafts" in November/December, 1970, managing editor Patricia J. MacKay sketched some of man's history with face coverings.

155

Facing It

by Patricia J. MacKay

Masks have a quality of magic and mystery about them. In society they become objects of beauty and disguise; they are presumed to have the ability, as at a costume ball or pre-lenten celebration, to free the wearer to indulge himself without fear of recognition. In religious ritual, the earliest of all dramatic experiences—whether chronologically or sociologically within any given cultural development, whether Greeks or present day tribesmen—primitive men have always made masks essential.

Masks have been used by medicine men (Shaman) in an effort to secure success in the hunt, to ward off disease, to cure sickness, to preserve (as in a Death Mask) features of a once living person. Some primitive people feel that they are safe from attack by the particular animal that they have chosen as a brother, or "bush soul," by wearing the mask, thereby assuming the identity of that animal. Masks have been instrumental in religion and war; they have made it easier to face the gods and have protected men from hostile environments.

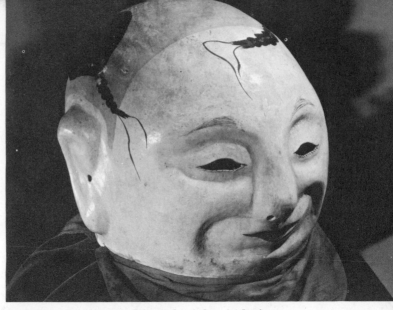

Tibetan monks wear paper maché masks (above) during ceremonies to chase out evil spirits and welcome the New Year. A 15th Century Japanese Noh mask (facing page, left), from the Tokyo National Museum, and a Peruvian mask enscribed on a gourd (facing page, right) were among the exhibits at the Museum of Contemporary Crafts' exhibition "Face Coverings."

As societies advance and drama is no longer inextricably incorporated into the structure of religion, masks come to serve other dramatic purposes. The Greeks used the mask to extend the magic of theatre. Constructed of painted and pierced canvas, the Greek mask enabled an actor to project his mood or character to the farthest seat in the theatre. For the Greek theatre the mask also became a method of expansion. The three actors could change masks (and with them characters), and thereby play many different parts. Masks continued to have a role in the drama of Rome, and the medieval mysteries and moralities. But by the rise of the *commedia dell' arte,* the full-face, rigid mask of the early Greeks had shrunk to a softer, half-face domino.

157

In the Orient, masks have followed much the same path as in the Occident—progressing from religious to broader uses. The No plays make use of 125 named varieties of faces representing the categories of old person, male, female, god or goddess, and devil or goblin.

A keynote of recent theatrical experimentation has been a "return to roots," getting back to basics by searching for

*Reminiscent of the New
Guinea Mudmen masks (pp.
164–165), though not included
in the Museum of Contemporary Crafts exhibition, is a
series of masks designed by
E. T. Kirby for a production
of "Ubu Roi." The rigid
textured headpieces, made of
self-hardening clay, cover the
entire face. Flexible jaws or
chin pieces, make them man-
ageable for the actors at the
State University of New York
in Binghamton, where de-
signer Kirby is a faculty member. He is also author of "The
Total Theatre."*

159

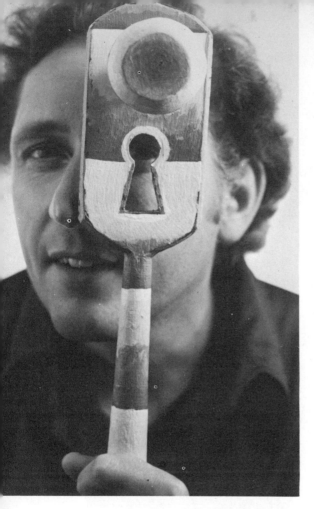

Tom Simpson designed some new face coverings in a contemporary idiom (left, above); Traditional face coverings include the Japanese Kabuki makeup (facing page, top right) and a beaded elephant dance costume from Cameroun (facing page, top left). Bob Hanson designed slide-projected masks (facing page, bottom).

160

the real meanings and experience of drama. Walter Kerr points out in an article contained in *Theatre 2,* entitled "God on the Gymnasium Floor" that "the theatre believing itself to be, in all of its older manifestation, dead, is seeking out a fresh identity, looking for a third coming. It remembers plainly that in its first two comings (Greek and Medieval) it came out of a religious or ceremonial impulse, out of a mythic rite and sometimes out of god-induced ecstacy. To find a new way of being itself, it must go back to its sources, beyond Euripides . . . into the dim intuited gropings by means of which flesh became spirit and spirit flesh."

If man is being forced by the dramatic experience to take another look, to re-evaluate himself and his action, could it be that the only way he will recognize "mythic" truths is when he does not recognize himself—when a mask prevents him from identifying with the character?

Other contemporary approaches in the exhibition included
Bob Hanson's slide-projected masks (above), Kathryn
Stoll's face outline (facing page, left), and Bruno Munari's
graphic cutouts (facing page, below).

165

*Masked for ceremonial occasions
are contemporary Mudmen
(top) from New Guinea, a
group of celebrants at a pre-
Lenten Carnival in Belgium
(middle, above), and Guate-
malan Indians portraying
Spanish conquistadores (below).*

Why did late 17th Century English play-goers wear masks to their playhouses? How did they believe that they would not be recognized? What does women's everyday street makeup represent to them—and to the men they may be trying to attract? What effects, beyond mere disguise, can this facial let's pretend produce in the theatre today? Others of our authors ask some of these same questions. Russell Graves helps to answer them in general terms by analyzing the basic psychological responses that masks can evoke. He traces the historical evolution and decay of masks, then discusses two main functions of masks as they have always been used by playwrights, directors, and performers. His isolating these phenomena makes a statement about contemporary society, as well as about contemporary theatre. And it suggests, by the very juxtaposition of the tradition of theatrical masks to the currently unmasked Environmental Theatre, that the way to make any polemic, propaganda, or guerrilla theatre—or any theatre about pure values—is inevitably through the use of mask or masks of some kind.

166

Russell Graves followed his service in World War II with a brief stint as a radio writer-director in New York, went to Dartmouth College as playwright-in-residence, and then back to Carnegie-Mellon to complete his B.F.A. and M.F.A. degrees. His plays have been produced at Dartmouth,

Carnegie-Mellon, Penn State, Cornell, North Carolina, and other universities. He is presently Professor of Dramatic Art at the University of North Carolina in Chapel Hill, where he was lighting designer for eight years before taking up his present duties as instructor of acting and directing.

The following article first appeared in "Theatre Crafts" magazine in January/ February 1971.

167

Heavy, stylized makeup can create the effect of a rigid mask (below) yet retain the Oriental theatre's pliant mask effect.

The Psychological Effects of Masks

by Russell Graves

Despite the recurring demands for greater realism in the modern theatre, playwrights and directors have regularly called for a return to the mask as a device that held out promise of infinite artistic rewards. Pirandello became so fascinated with it that he accepted it as the great metaphor in most of his major plays. O'Neill, Brecht, Genet, and others have used the mask more literally than Pirandello as a way of resolving problems they encountered when confronted with the barefaced actor. Few designers have not toyed at one time or another with the implication of the masked human face.

The difficulty is that very few of us understand the way in which the mask worked in those periods when it was a

A rigid half mask (above) is part of the commedia dell'arte tradition.

primary element of production. In order to answer what has attracted performers to the use of mask, it is necessary to trace the recurring decay of the mask as a theatrical device. In its earliest stages, the mask is usually rigid and covers the entire face. As time goes on it tends to develop in either one of two directions: it covers less of the face, or it is softened into makeup and becomes more pliant.

169

Starting as a device for isolating the performer from the world of everyday reality, the mask eventually becomes less and less committed to this ideal and tries to get closer to the appearances of individual men. The progression, then, is from the unnatural freezing of a single human characteristic (e.g., avarice, lust, sloth) to the revealing of an entire spectrum of human characteristics—an even greater naturalism of representation. This is achieved at the cost of abstraction, generalization, and isolation of the characteristics of mankind.

The trend from the hard mask to the soft (i.e., the bare face, made up or not) is visible in both the ancient and modern world, and it is always accompanied by a corresponding softening of the content and manner of the performance. Particularly in the *commedia dell' arte* did this softening process take place. The hard-hitting, unflinching, bawdy, and broad *commedia* of the 16th and 17th Centuries turned into the lovely, but effete pantomime of Deburau's Pierrot. The hard mask had become softened to the clown makeup, which eventually became as pliant as Charlie Chaplin's greatly magnified and magnificently expressive face. After Deburau, after Chaplin, there was no place to go, and the mask disappeared from the theatre entirely, only to rise later in another of its Phoenix-like reincarnations.

There have been two main functions of the mask in its great periods of ascendance:

1. *The mask served to isolate a human characteristic from its setting in a total personality.* The familiar masks of the past and present have represented only one characteristic of the human being. Hamlet is intriguing as a complex personality, but cannot be imagined masked, except in a very complex, Pirandellian way. But Oedipus also is intriguing as the epitome of intellectual curiosity driven to the point of no return. When Oedipus' mask is removed so too is the magnificent isolation of his *ideé fixe* removed. He becomes "merely" human, no longer making the transcendent statement he did when the actor's face was concealed.

In the *commedia dell' arte,* the isolation of avarice in Pantalone or of intellectual pretension in the Dottore is completely crystallized in their masks. The actor cannot escape into the complexities of personality. In a sense, he

Masks can be used to make a distinction between characters with whom the audience is asked to identify and those about whom they are to be objective, as in the University of North Carolina's production of "The Beggar's Opera (below).

Masks can be both scenic costume and disembodied spirits as they watch over a scene from "The Battle of the Carnival and Lent" (top). With different effects, isolated masks, masked characters, and a momentarily unmasked character (above) combine during a scene in "The Good Woman of Setzuan."

is the prisoner of the mask, and he must play out his part in terms of the statement *it* makes, rather than in terms of some complex of emotions that go beyond that statement.

We can see individual characteristics under the microscope, and we are able to probe all of their implications without the confusion of "but, on the other hand" subleties necessarily implicit in the unmasked face, mirroring as it does all the intricacies of the human soul.

2. *The mask places a barrier between the actor and the spectator.* An aesthetic barrier, if you will. The spectator is discouraged from, indeed he is not permitted to identify with the character. He can only study him objectively. When freed of the responsibility for identification, he is also freed

In Oriental theatre, the mask or mask-like makeup helps to isolate the characteristics of the individual, as in "The Good Woman of Setzuan" (above). A mixture of masks and unmasked faces (below) creates the impression of a larger cast as well as of hovering spirits.

Traditional half masks of the commedia dell'arte (top, left and right, and above left) create a special mask effect. Through highly disciplined physical control and careful lighting, an unmasked face can act as a mask (above, right).

The hard-playing hard mask of commedia dell'arte is used in combination with the soft-mask makeup of the Pierrot pantomime (above).

from the need to defend his own ego by withdrawing some of his emotional commitment for fear of psychological trauma.

The spectator at the masked performance is a god watching men of more limited range of emotion than himself as they are driven to the limits of their humanity. He is freed from fear by the presence of the mask. Such devices of the *commedia* as having a character eat flies or eat his own brains are impossible to perform successfully unless the actor is masked and the audience is reassured by the consequent removal of events from everyday reality.

When the mask is softened, the spectator begins to guard himself from shock, and the closer it gets to the appearance of everyday man, the less free he feels to surrender his self-protective instincts. The unmasked actor is the occasion for a war within the spectator between his desire to accept the character as human and his need to protect his own emotional being.

174

Each of the two theatres (i.e., masked and unmasked) provides specific kinds of resources for the performer, including the director and playwright. When the mask is not used, the spectator is encouraged to identify subjectively with the character and to work through his entire range of emotion with him. When the actor is masked, on the other hand, the spectator is freed from the trauma associated with identification, freed to observe and experience.

Today again, masks have been resurrected by playwrights and directors and actors who feel that in some way they must eliminate the complexity of individual men to make a statement about Man.

*Irene Corey's truly inspired and unforget-
table makeup for church theatre and children's theatre productions has, in the main,
been masks made of highly stylized makeup
(see page 94). Here, she discusses the uses,
effects, design, and fabrication of actual
masks made of sculptured paper for a production of Eugene O'Neill's "The Great
God Brown." These sculptural but not
papier maché masks may be not unlike the
archetypal masks of unpainted linen
that Thespis legendarily introduced to the
theatre. The ambiguity and mystery of
Irene Corey's half masks, with their
simplified planes of almost archaic force
were emphasized during the performance,
since the masks were changed from act to
act, each successive one aging in a semi-
realistic yet surreal progression. Designer
Corey describes step-by-step her method of
pattern making, mask cutting and fitting,
kinds of paper, gluing, fixing, and final
painting as a guide for other mask makers.*

*Besides designing for the Marjorie Lyons
Theatre at Centenary College in Shreveport, Louisiana, for the past 10 years, she
has, with her husband Orlin Corey, produced and designed for their professional
company, The Everyman Players, which is
based in Pineville, Kentucky, during the
summers. The company has toured extensively in Canada and this country, and in
England, Belgium, and South Africa, with
productions of the religious dramas "The*

175

Book of Job," "The Romans by St. Paul,"
and also with such children's theatre productions as "The Tortoise and the Hare,"
and "Reynard the Fox." Their most recent
production was an episodic and brilliant
version of "A Pilgrim's Progress."

The following article was first published
in "Theatre Crafts" in May/June, 1969.

176

To Make a Paper Mask

by Irene Corey

At Centenary College in Shreveport, Louisiana, the undergraduate students were well into the opening scene of Eugene O'Neill's *The Great God Brown*. In the fifth row center the president's wife leaned to her husband and whispered, "I thought they were supposed to wear masks." "I thought so, too," he replied. About that time Dion removed his mask.

Since the first primitive "actor" stepped out from the ritual group to put one on, man has responded to the mystery that wearing a mask evokes. The Greeks realized the potential of the mask as an enlargement of self—an extension of the individual actor's powers. Even today's know-it-all man occasionally succumbs to being momentarily transported via another guise on Mardi Gras or All Hallows' Eve.

Playwrights have never forgotten the use of the mask. They keep returning to it as Archibald MacLeish did in *J.B.* for the roles of God and Satan, or for the Indians and various characters in Genet's *The Blacks*. Eugene O'Neill was fascinated with the mask and even though he wrote during the theatre's most realistic phase, he suggested its use for the puppet-like creatures of Fifth Avenue in *The Hairy Ape* and carried it to great extremes in *Lazarus Laughed*. (Although O'Neill himself did not prescribe their use, *The Emperor Jones* could be staged magnificently by using primitive masks.)

The completed mask for Dion (left) is also worn by Billy in Act III. Cybele's mask (facing page) was inspired by the sensuous smile of an archaic Greek statue.

178

However, in *The Great God Brown*, O'Neill wove the use of the mask inextricably into the fabric of the play. By making changeable the exterior "face" that his characters present to the world, he was able to reveal beneath, the condition of their inner selves, thus allowing the audience to follow several dimensions of character development. We see the facade that the character presents to the world— as he wishes to be seen—externally represented by a mask. By a series of masks we see the aging process brought on by time and internal pressures. Finally, when all the masks have been stripped away, the inner self, the true state of the soul of the character is revealed.

Technically, the most difficult problem is to make the convention of frequent mask changes acceptable to the audience without interrupting the flow of the play. In this case, flow is hampered by O'Neill's use of the realistic tradition of repeated set changes from offices to homes. Yet the change in locale is incidental to his main theme, which concerns the change in individuals.

In the early planning sessions for our production at Centenary College, we searched for a plausible idea for a unit set. When I reread the script for clues, I became aware that scene after scene, whether a wharf, a living room, or

Lined up on shelves are all of Irene Corey's masks for "The Great God Brown" (left) with the mask for Billy Brown in Act III, Scene I (above).

an office, had one aspect in common: O'Neill's indication of an arrangement that suggested a courtroom situation with a bench and a witness stand. The director, Phillip Anderson, accepted my suggestion that this play, concerned with the probing of man's interactions and motivations might be set in a universal courtroom; that the "jury" be made up of the minor characters—the committee men, draftsmen, the three sons, the secretary, etc. Masking would extend to them, as it is only their exterior selves that O'Neill outlines.

The setting, designed by Ken Holamon, was multi-leveled with the traditional elements of a courtroom stylized, exaggerating the size of the judge's bench. This setting enabled the "trial" to continue suspended in space, uninterrupted by scene changes. Characters stepped out of the "jury" to assume roles in the enactment of events which formulated "testimony."

Dion's suffering was inspired by the agonized face of a young captain in Viet-Nam who had survived a harrowing experience with his men; his spiritualism came from the face of a priest; his poetic revolt from the sensitive image of Jean-Louis Barrault. Billy Brown's disintegration into materialism was found in the set of the mouth of a censured senator and the horizontal brow of a businessman. From a teen-age fashion model came the vapid, "ideal" beauty of Margaret; from an archaic Greek statue came Cybele's

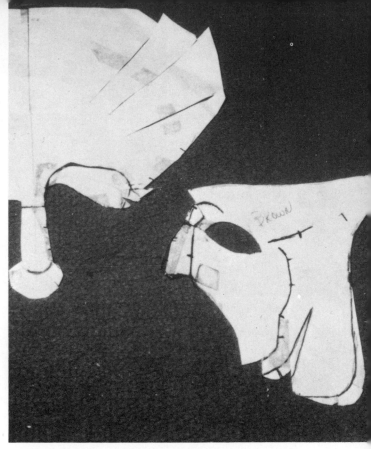

*The origi-
nal paper
pattern
for Billy
Brown's
mask in
Act III
(right).*

sensuous smile and classic loveliness. All these characteristics were amalgamated into designs for either makeup
plots or half-masks. The half-masks extended below the
cheek bone, leaving the mouth free.

How then, to make the masks? They must go on and off
easily. They must be durable. The thickness of most media
does not allow a smooth transition from cheek to face. I
decided to try paper sculpture. Although I was not sure it
would hold up, I knew it would create sharp, clear planes,
and would be light to wear. By extending the mask to include the crown of the head, hair also was styled in the
same manner. The resultant tension between the back of
the crown and the cheek held the mask smoothly in place.

Patterns were created by smoothing heavy brown paper
across the forehead and down against the nose. By feeling
and marking, the bridge of the nose and the indentations

The final mask pattern for Billy Brown was transferred to Wattman watercolor paper (above).

under the brow were tentatively located. The area above the forehead became the crown and was slit into radiating strips which curved over the top of the head and fastened at the back.

After the first pattern was fastened onto the head with pins, a second piece of paper was smoothed across the cheekbone toward the side of the nose and folded upward to the section of the first pattern which formed the bridge of the nose. Above the cheek, the paper was creased and slit to form the eye socket and to connect to the brow of the first pattern. After the eye-hole was cut out, further alterations were made to refine the facial features into simplified planes.

During the fitting stage, all pieces were temporarily taped together. After having been marked, they were untaped, laid flat, scored, creased and re-fitted. The corrected pattern was transferred to Wattman watercolor paper.

A final fitting was made on each actor with the mask in taped-up form. All gluing was done with white adhesive— such as Elmer's. Hair was formed by cutting the paper into strips, and then scraping one side with a knife to achieve a curled effect. (The paper will maintain its shape and can be glued into place.) Eyelids and eyebrows were added later. The finished mask was painted inside with two

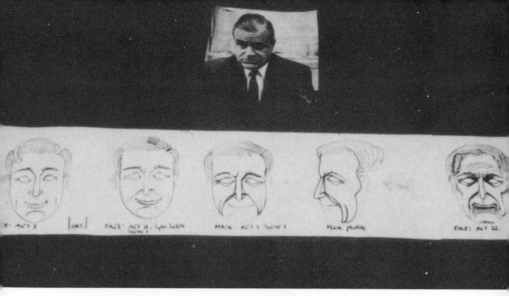

A photograph was the prototype for the final makeup and mask design for Billy Brown in Act III (above).

coats of full strength glue, and then sprayed with clear plastic. The outside had a ground of rust colored acrylic paint on which features and hair were painted. Working time ran approximately 12 hours per mask. Makeup was mixed to blend with the color of the masks.

In action, the masks held up through three weeks of rehearsal and performance, were astonishingly effective and would have lasted many months. We had expected them to look "mask-like" and to be accepted as such. We had made the eerie discovery that once the actor donned the mask, it so thoroughly became a part of him that he was instantly transformed. The masks fulfilled their ideal goal without calling attention to themselves. They heightened the inner emotion portrayed by the actor, and they helped him to project clearly his outer character.

183

184

Among the many boons that the theatre derives from newly developed plastics, the making of masks—human, animal, or fantastic—is a notable beneficiary. Plastics have brought greater ease of casting techniques, greater variety of molding materials, and greater potential uses for casting in general. Besides masks, these new materials and techniques can be applied, virtually without alteration, to the construction of those replicas of various body parts that the theatre requires in its gleefully gory way to serve as severed members—heads, hands, legs. Casting these artificial parts is similar to the construction of those prosthetic facial fragments that are used for builtup character makeups. Making comfortable, well fitting armor starts with these same techniques, and all sorts of other props and architectural details of settings—balusters, columns, statuary—can be cast by the same methods, with the same new plastics. To theatre technicians, then, this basic methodology is essential.

As a detailed how-to, step-by-step description of these techniques and their special application to mask making, the following article by Alan G. Billings guides us every step of the way in making life casts as negative molds—to ensure fit and comfort of the inner surface of a theatre masks—then in making positive molds for the exterior surface of the mask itself.

Especially clear is author Billings' methodology on separating the negative mold and preparing it for the positive. He provides warnings and, in case we neglect to heed them, suggestions on how to make corrections along the way. He also offers alternate methods, views on alternate materials, and additional uses of casting.

Alan G. Billings has been scenic and lighting designer for the Ogunquit Playhouse in Maine, the Southbury Playhouse in Connecticut, the Atlanta Municipal Theatre, and the Southern Ballet in Atlanta. He received his B.F.A. degree from the University of Georgia, an M.F.A. from Carnegie-Mellon University, and a Ph.D. from the University of Illinois. He currently teaches scene and lighting design at the University of Michigan.

The following article was first published in "Theatre Crafts" in October, 1969.

185

Masks and full heads (above) can be easily and effectively cast with flexible foam.

Casting Masks of Flexible Foam

by Alan G. Billings

In this day of technical marvels, theatre technicians are continually on the look-out for new materials for the construction of properties demanded by the play. Many plays call for special properties that require precise shapes: *Macbeth* and *The Bacchae*, for example, each require that the severed head of one of the principal characters be brought on stage, and naturally these prop heads should be a close likeness to the actors; other productions may require the use of masks for the cast. In the past, such props and masks have generally been made of plaster or papier-mache. Today there are two new materials that are in many ways superior —polystyrene and flexible latex rubber; these, combined with the old technique of casting from a mold, offer a practical and easy process for producing lightweight and flexible properties and masks.

Rigid polystyrene or styrofoam has been in use as a scenic material for several years. It is usually bought in rigid sheets or planks that are easily cut, gouged, and carved. However, when working with the casting technique,

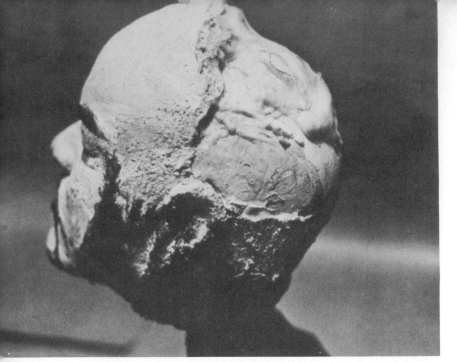

A foam face mask is made into a complete head by attaching it to a styrofoam wig form (above), which is later covered with a wig. During the casting of the negative mold of an actor's face, soda straws permit breathing (facing page).

it is necessary to begin with the basic materials—two liquids that expand to form styrofoam when mixed together. These liquids conform to the shape of the container and retain that shape when hardened. Polystyrene can be produced in varying degrees of density and flexibility depending upon the composition of the original liquids. A flexible foam casting material has many advantages over rigid foam, and especially over plaster: the form is more easily removed from rigid plaster molds; a form cast in foam is lighter weight; and a flexible form will not break or chip.

188

The only practical solution to the problem of the severed heads required for *Macbeth* and *The Bacchae* is first to make a negative life cast mold of the actor's face and then a positive form from that negative mold. The negative mold is generally cast from plaster of paris or Negocoll. The positive can be cast from a number of materials: either papier-mache, plaster of paris, celastic (all of which have the drawbacks of being either fragile, heavy, or poorly textured), or polystyrene and latex rubber, which are lighter, stronger, flexible, and have a flesh-like texture.

Plaster casting is not difficult to master. Professional theatre technicians have long used this substance in constructing property and scenery equipment. To cast a solid object such as a head, only the negative mold is needed, and the positive form becomes the head. With the use of both the negative and positive casts in making masks, the inside of the mask can be form-fitted to any portion of the actor's face while the outside can be formed with as much detail and intricacy as desired.

Casting techniques

In most cases, plaster of paris can be used to cast the negative mold. Surgical plaster is useful when it is necessary for the cast to set quickly. But to cast forms other than the human face, a flexible material must be used. I recommend a liquid rubber latex that comes in either one or two components, that can be mixed together and poured over the objects to be cast. The rubber vulcanizes at room temperature and can then be stripped off the object. To cast a body mold, I suggest something flexible such as Negocoll.

When making a life-like cast of the face, it is important to pay particular attention to the preparation of materials and the subject. Assemble the following materials: plaster of paris, petroleum jelly, cotton, surgical gauze, two soda straws, rubber bald pate wig, base or a nylon stocking to cover the hair, plastic mixing bowl, water, mixing stick, clean-up rags, sponges, smock or work clothes, and several pasteboard strips (2" x 7"). Although it is possible for one person to make the cast, it is preferable to have one or two assistants.

The actor whose face is to be cast applies petroleum jelly to his face and all the parts which might come in contact with the plaster; eyelashes, brows, and the hair line should be carefully coated to prevent sticking. Because the hairline is seldom reproduced, the actor can cover his hair with a rubber bald-pate wig or a nylon stocking. Small strips of facial tissue or gauze that will serve as an extra precaution can be placed over his eyebrows, lashes, and sideburns.

190

The actor lies on a narrow table during the procedure, so that the technician can easily reach both sides of his head. To permit easy breathing, a soda straw is placed in each nostril and held in place with cotton. Cotton might also be placed in the ears to guard against plaster drips. (See Figure 1.)

When the actor is comfortable and can breathe easily, the next step is to mix the plaster. It is not nesessary to mix all the plaster at one time. A double handful of plaster is placed in a mixing bowl, and a small amount of water is added a little at a time; these are mixed easily until the consistency of whipped cream or soft dough is reached. The more it is

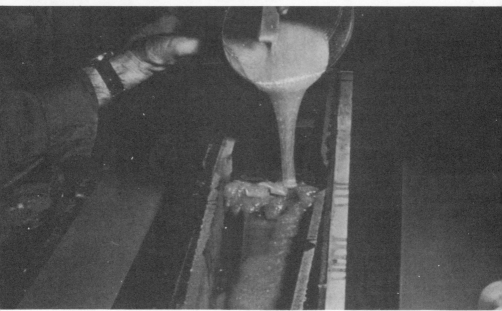

Balusters and other architectural elements used in settings, as well as other props, also are now made with flexible foam. Latex liquid is used to protect the original before it is used as a positive for a negative mold (top). Additional latex is then poured over the original in a box to make a mold (below).

stirred, the faster it will begin to set and harden. Too thick a mixture will not conform to the contours of the face and will cause air pockets; too thin a mixture will run off. If the mixture tends to drip off the sides of the face, strips of pasteboard can be held to the sides of the face as dikes. If the original amount of plaster is insufficient, more can be mixed and the process continued until the mold is at least two inches thick all over. It is important that the actor not move his face during the casting process, because any movement will cause distortion of the cast's features.

The cast should be allowed to dry for at least fifteen minutes before removal from the actor's face. To remove the cast, it is necessary to get air between the face and the cast. This can be done by having the actor exhale through his mouth and by stretching the flesh back at the sides of the face. The cast is then slipped down toward the chin and off.

Although a plaster cast is fragile at all times, it is most fragile before it has completely dried and should be handled with extreme care. The inside of the cast should be checked for air pockets and irregularities, any facial tissue or gauze should be removed, and the straws should be clipped short or removed. Air pockets can be filled by rubbing in wet plaster that is the consistency of wood putty. After repairs have been made, the cast should be permitted to cure over night. The negative mold resulting from the preceding process is very useful for a number of jobs. A plaster positive form cast from the negative mold can be used as a form in which to build false beards and latex prosthesis. The severed head prop also can be cast from this negative mold.

192

Casting the Positive Form

Before casting the positive form, the inside of the negative mold must be treated to prevent the new plaster from sticking. The negative mold must be coated with shellac. When it is dry, a coating of petroleum jelly or household paraffin wax is applied to all the surfaces that will come into contact with the new plaster. The wax is melted and applied to the surface with a small brush, and it will harden as soon as it touches the plaster. Care must be taken to cover the entire surface of the mold completely without building up a thick layer, because too thick a layer can cause the features to become less distinct.

Once the surface treatment has been completed, the mold should be placed in a horizontal position and braced to prevent it from tipping when the plaster is poured. The plaster is mixed in the same manner as the negative mold, using care so that it reaches into all the crevices and no air pockets form. While the plaster is still wet, one or two lengths of heavy wire or flexible metal strips should be partially embedded into it. The wire acts as a handle for removing the positive form and for attaching it to a support. The plaster should dry overnight before removal from the mold. If both the negative and the positive are made of rigid plaster, there may be some difficulty in separating the two. If they cannot be separated by gently pulling and rocking the positive form, the negative can be carefully split with a chisel along the long axis in line with the nose and later rejoined, if necessary. If the negative mold has any extreme undercuts, such as the mouth or nose, it would be easier to split the mold before casting and hold it together with rubber bands or tape. There is less difficulty in separating the two forms if a flexible material, such as rubber latex or polystyrene foam, is used to form the positive.

To cast with flexible material, the negative plaster mold is prepared in the same way as casting with plaster. The first layer of the positive form is made of the same type of rubber latex as is used in makeup for attaching beards. The latex is dabbed on one layer at a time with cotton, allowing each layer to dry thoroughly before adding the next. At least four layers are necessary to develop an exterior skin for the form. The latex skin should not be removed from the plaster cast.

193

The major portion of the positive form is formed by mixing two liquids together, a plastic foam and a foaming agent. The two liquids are mixed vigorously for about 45 seconds and then poured into a mold. The mixture begins to foam and expands to fill the crevices of the mold. Within 20 minutes, the foam will have reached its maximum volume. Any excess can be cut off; if more is needed, it can be mixed and added. The liquid will expand to approximately twice its original volume.

The Rest of the Head

Up to this point, the problem of reproducing only the actor's face has been considered, but a prop head must be complete on top and in back also. Since the top and the back of the prop head will be covered with a wig, there is no need for any great detail in the form. The major portion of the back can be simulated with a styrofoam wig block. Before the liquid in the mold has reached its full volume and begins to harden, the wig block is carefully aligned with the face mold. As the liquid foam expands, it will foam up around the wig block and any excess can be trowelled smoothly up and around its side. However, it will be necessary to tape or tie the wig block down, to prevent the rising foam from pushing it out of position. Once the foam has hardened and is no longer sticky, the wig block can be carefully removed from the mold. The joint between the face and the head not covered by the wig may need trimming with scissors or building up with rubber latex and cotton. The face can now be made up to match the actor's. With the proper application of makeup or paint, the head can be made as realistic, gory, or stylized as desired. Because it is lightweight and flexible, there is no danger of its being dropped and broken.

Soft, pliable masks can also be made by using the same techniques and materials. Masks can be cast as large, full head shells—as for large animal heads—or smaller character or fantasy masks that conform more closely to the actor's face and head size.

194

Animal Masks

Large animal head masks must first be modelled in clay, and then a negative plaster mold made as described above. From this the positive mask is cast. If only one mask is to be made, this method can be too time consuming to be practical. On the other hand, more intricate detail can be produced by casting from a negative mold.

When the negative mold has set, the positive is removed and any built-up clay is removed from either the positive or the negative mold. In order to make a mask that fits perfectly to the actor's face, both the positive cast of the actor's face and the negative cast of the mask will be used in the final casting step.

The severed head of John The Baptist is served up to Salome as
the prize for her dance of the seven veils in the Metropolitan
Opera Company production of the Richard Strauss opera. Birgit
Nilsson is seen as Salome (above) with Irene Dalis as Herodias
in the background.

In the same manner as already described, dab on at least three layers of latex makeup adhesive to both the negative mold of the mask and the positive mold of the actor's face. When the skin has dried, arrange a support which permits the positive mold to be supported above and inside the negative mold. There should be at least ⅜ to ½ inch clearance between the two molds. Into this space will be poured the flexible plastic foam liquid that will form the major bulk of the mask. Care should be taken to align what will be the eye, nose, and mouth openings. Some sort of key or guide marks should be arranged so that the positive mold can be removed for pouring and replaced in the exact position.

The positive mold is now removed to permit easy pouring. The two liquids are mixed and poured into the negative mold. Then the positive mold is replaced, making sure that it hangs in the correct position. The positive mold should be tied down to prevent the rising foam from pushing it out of place. Once the foam has set, the molds may be removed, using care so that the latex skin is separated from the mold and not the foam center. Again, it may be necessary to split the negative cast to remove the mask. Once removed, the excess can be trimmed and the eye and nostril holes opened with scissors. The same liquid latex used for the skin can be used to make any necessary repairs. Coloring can be done with regular makeup or spray paint. A full head mask can best be made in two sections, front and back, that are then sewn or glued together. Other features, such as hair or horns, can be cast separately and attached later.

Other Uses

The use of plastic foam and the technique of casting is not limited to the making of severed heads or masks. It can be useful in many instances where lightweight material or an exact replica of a form is needed. Plaster reproductions of the human body are useful as forms for making armor. The important points of casting are that the surface to be cast must be prepared to prevent sticking, and undercuts must be cast either in two parts or with flexible material. Other steps of the process can be varied to suit the individual problem. Materials can be obtained from local hardware stores, hobby shops, or stage makeup suppliers. The intricacy of form and the application of techniques are limited only by the imagination and skill of the technician.

No verbal description of an involved, multistep methodology—however complete and detailed—can create the totality or the actuality of that process. For someone who has not had the practical experience—the physical exposure to the process in operation—a description can be merely a mystifying enumeration of exercises. Two descriptions of the same cast-molding and maskmaking process, therefore, can hardly complete the education of a technician who has never actually made a mask in this way, any more than reading two recipes can make an expert cook. Craftsmanship derives from frequent repetition with constant care. But through the multiple exposure of this and the preceding article, we create a rare comparative view of current casting technology and molding materials.

The following article emphasizes the importance of careful preparatory steps; the author provides simplifications and elaborations of various segments of the process such as measuring, preventative precautions, and reinforcing. He recommends different materials for making molds. With these additional details and refinements, mask makers will find the built-up chamois commedia dell'arte masks that Peter Maslan designed to be neatly informative exemplars to supplement their own methodologies.

Peter Maslan worked with the Oregon Shakespeare Festival as property master and assistant to the stage designer. He de-

197

signed settings for "Joe Egg," "Summer-tree," and "The Initiation" at the Seattle Repertory Theatre, and also worked as designer and technical director at the Sacramento Civic Theatre. He holds an M.A. from San Francisco State College and is presently designer/technical director at Allan Hancock College, Santa Maria, California.

The following article was first published in "Theatre Crafts" November/December issue, 1971.

198

About Face: Chamois Commedia Masks

by Peter Maslan

It is not often that a theatre designer or technician has the opportunity, as I did, to work in a new theatre during its first season. The Angus Bowmer Theatre of the Oregon Shakespearean Festival in Ashland, Oregon, which opened in 1969 is a single chamber structure designed by architects Kirk, Wallace, McKinley & Associates. There is an aura of oneness or nearness to the on-stage action from the first row in the house all the way to the last. So there was a need for totally credible props with maximum reality and detail.

For our production of Moliere's *The Imaginary Invalid*, one particular task for the property master was to construct a set of *commedia dell'arte* masks for the "mechanicals" to be included in the play. Not only did the masks have to be realistic, but they had to be lightweight and formfitting so they wouldn't hinder the actors.

In addition, they had to look like they were made of leather; and they were to be worn throughout the entire two and a half hours of the play. During this time there was only one chance for the mechanicals to get off stage, remove their masks, and take a breather. Anyone who has worn a poorly fitted mask can sympathize with the problem: every sensitive point around the temples and forehead turns into a dull, throbbing pain area under a too-tight-fitting mask.

The solution to the fitting problem was to form individual masks on casts of each actor's face. In this way, every

Chamois half masks, molded by Peter Maslan, were worn by commedia dell'arte mechanicals (above) in the Oregon Shakespeare Festival's production of Moliere's "The Imaginary Invalid."

part of the mask that touched the face would fit naturally. To get the leathery look, we found that chamois skin dipped in glue and stretched over a celastic base was the most realistic.

Making a Negative Mold

The first step is to make a collar of upson board around the head so that work can be localized to the area needed. In order to have an exact cross section of the cheek lines, chin, temples, and forehead, a wire loop can be made to fit the exact contours of the head. The best type of wire to use is ⅛ inch solder because it is so flexible, yet once bent retains its shape.

When the shape of the loop is transferred onto the upson board, it is important to center the loop crossways on the board. To provide maximum comfort for the subject the outline should be placed so that the chin area is only two or three inches from the bottom of the board.

Once the hole has been cut out, the edges are then sanded. By trimming and sanding, the board may be fitted exactly onto the subject's head. The subject should apply a thin layer of cold cream (slightly heavier around the eyebrows and lashes) to his face.

A sheet of plastic stretched across the forehead with the bottom edge placed just below the hairline allows for an easier separation of the cast from the face, as well as a smoother area on the top of the cast itself. The plastic sheeting must be kept tight across the forehead as the board is put into place. It may be necessary to support the board with rags or tissue paper wedged between the board and the surface on which the subject is lying.

The next step is to apply the negative mold. The material we used at the Angus Bowmer Theatre is Jel-Trate, which can be purchased at any dental or medical supply house. Unlike the traditional morticians moulage, it cannot be used over again; however, it does have its own advantages. It is mixed with water, and since it does not have to be heated, it is more comfortable on a subject's face. Since setting speed is determined by the water temperature, it can be mixed to set up quite rapidly. This also means a minimum of discomfort to the subject. We have found the material to be most successful when mixed to the consistency of porridge.

201

The person making the cast should first grease his hands, then apply the Jel-Trate to the subject's forehead, then the chin, mouth and cheeks. It is a good idea to tell the subject just where you are working so he can relax that part of his face, and avoid getting a mouthful of Jel-Trate.

Some mask makers feel it is necessary to place straws in the subject's nostrils or mouth to facilitate breathing. We found that this changed the shape of the nostrils, or gave the lips a pucker in the final cast. By carefully applying the Jel-Trate around the nostrils and over the tip of the nose, as well as bringing it over the upper lip just to the nostrils, enough area is sufficiently defined so that the nose can be accurately shaped with just a minimal amount of carving on the final product.

When the mold material has set, surgical plaster strips are dipped in water, and placed on the surface of the mold. These strips of gauze, impregnated with fine plaster, become like instant plaster of paris when dipped in water. This application serves as reinforcement and as a supportive superstructure for the Jel-Trate, once the mold is upside down. The plaster strips should be built up around the nose opening to add maximum support when moving the cast.

"Anyone who has worn a poorly fitted mask can sympathize with the problem: every sensitive point around the temples and forehead turns into a dull, throbbing pain area under a too-tight-fitting mask."

"*The solution . . . was to form individual masks on plaster casts of each actor's face. In this way, every part of the mask that touched the face would fit naturally.*"

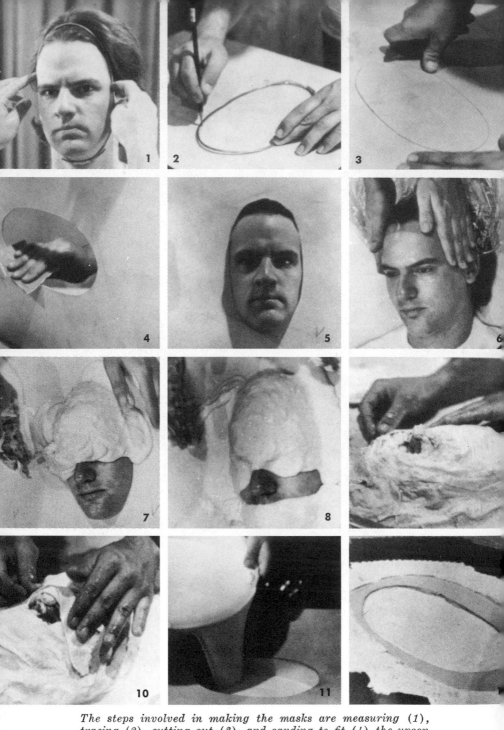

*The steps involved in making the masks are measuring (1),
tracing (2), cutting out (3), and sanding to fit (4) the upson
board used as a base on which to build the mask (5). Over a
hair-protecting plastic sheet (6), first Jel-Trate (7, 8), then
moistened plaster bandage strips (9, 10) form the negative
mold into which quick-set dental plaster (11) let set (12).*

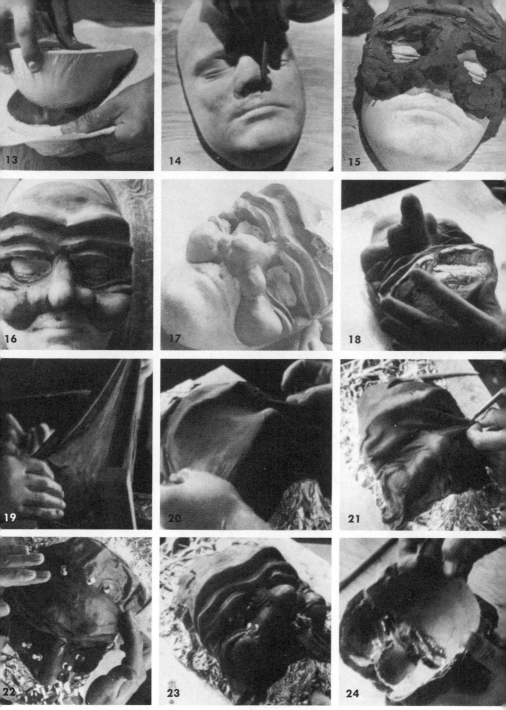

The plaster cast separates from the mold (13), imperfections are fixed (14), and a harlequin mask of clay is
formed and sculpted (15, 16). Tinfoil is carefully applied
to the mask (17, 18), torn celastic, then chamois dipped in
heated glue (19) are applied (20). Eye slits are cut (21),
character lines and wrinkles formed (22, 23). The mask is
loosened from the clay face (24).

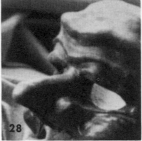

Mask edges are trimmed (25), painted black (26) and felt applied with hot melt glue (27) to produce an individually molded commedia dell'arte mask (28).

After the plaster strips have set, the mold can be "popped" from the subject's face. This is best done by having the subject support the mold against his face until he can get into a kneeling position. Then by simply leaning over, the mold will fall away.

The mold is now ready to be cast. The nose opening should be stopped up with clay. It is important to leave enough of a depression in the clay so that there is sufficient plaster to carve the rest of the nose. Quick set dental plaster saves time and adds strength to the cast.

Once set, the plaster cast separates easily from the mold, which can now be discarded. When the plaster has cured, the nose can be shaped with a clay or plaster carving tool. Imperfections such as positive cast air bubbles, eyebrows and hairline ridges should be sanded away.

Making the Mask

With the use of this cast plaster face, it is now possible to make an exact, form fitting mask. The mask is carved out of clay which has been applied over the face, cast to assure an exact fit of the finished mask over the actor's face.

Over a layer of tin foil, carefully applied to the clay, a layer of Celastic is applied. Torn pieces of medium grade Celastic should be used. It is worked into the creases and crevices of the mold with a wooden sculpting tool.

Once the Celastic has hardened, it becomes a strong base over which to stretch the chamois skin. This is the final layer of the mask. First, the chamois is moistened and squeezed dry. It is then dipped into heated animal skin glue which should be the consistency of milk. Excess glue is squeezed from the chamois which is then stretched over the mold.

Cross slits are cut in the chamois where eye holes will be. The flaps are pressed into the eye depressions of the mold. The chamois is further stretched using push pins to hold it tightly in place. As the chamois is stretched, wrinkles in the skin will appear. These can be utilized to accentuate the character of the mask in such a way that "smile wrinkles" may be formed around the eyes and cheek bones. The prominence of a nose such as El Capitan's can be achieved by forming wrinkles around the nostrils.

When the chamois has completely dried, the clay mold can be pried from the plaster cast. Then the clay and tinfoil are peeled from the Celastic and chamois mask.

The mask is trimmed and the edges are sanded. It is a good idea to paint the back of the mask with a black acrylic; this provides a protective coating against the moisture of makeup or perspiration. Strips of felt are glued around the eye holes and the mask edge to assure a more comfortable fit.

207

The finished result is a light-weight *commedia dell'arte* mask of leather with a Celastic base—formfitted to the individual actor's face.

*From his punning title onwards, Randy
Echols' informal fireside chat about the
mythology of masks brings us a smattering
of quotations from critics outside the
theatre and a homey rambling on the
backgrounds and meanings of masks. His
essay is more anthropological than theatre
oriented. Randy Echols is concerned with
the uses of masks against society,
masks for shyness, and masks of light; he
considers the function of helmets as masks,
of dominoes as masks, of eyeglasses as
masks. His is a search along the boundaries
of whatever might conceivably be considered as a mask, in order to throw new
light on our uses of them in traditional
theatre.*

*Randy Echols has held virtually every
kind of job in the theatre except that of playwright. In the past years he has, with his
wife, concentrated on mask making for the
theatre and for theatrical occasions.*

*The following article was first published
in "Theatre Crafts" in July/August, 1967.*

I Am a Chimera

by Randy Echols

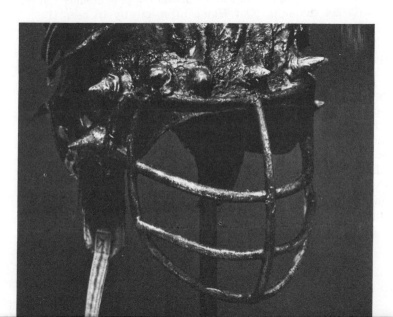

When P. G. Wodehouse said "it rankled, of course but we woosters can wear the mask," we knew precisely what he meant. Indeed, it is not too much to say that most of us wear some sort of mask all the time. We are many things to many people. If Dr. Freud is to be believed, we wear masks even in sleep and hide in symbols. It is possible that no one has had a true or fixed identity since we—mistakenly though it may be—crawled out of the sea and cried "Land Ho."

Be that as it may, the actors in ancient classical drama and the primitive tribes since pre-history were and are wiser. For one thing, wearing a mask of leather, wood, woven straw, feathers, cloth, paper, or just paint saves a lot of wear and tear on facial muscles. You can think your own thoughts, even sneer, without getting caught. You can go through the most grueling of monkey-drills, as an actor in a dull play or as a witch doctor with a leaden and unresponsive congregation, and come out feeling refreshed, even sassy. On another level, a mask may provide an escape from shyness or fear, or it may be just plain fun.

Painted masks include those of primitive ritual, oriental opera, and drama. The best known to us today are those of the circus clown, including—if you don't mind my stretching a point—the painted-on spectacles of Bobby Clark and Groucho's painted on moustache. For cloth masks, one might even include the bandanas of the bandits in *The Great Train Robbery*.

Some years ago, my wife and I presented puppet shows in a little art center in New Hampshire—mostly to keep the children away from the grown-ups while they considered whether or not to buy this painting or sculpture, this pot, that piece of silver, or this wooden bowl.

Each time the children would come backstage after a performance and want to see what made the wind and thunder, and what it was that made the terrible noise of Grandfather falling downstairs. All the sound effects were handmade and run by our own children as stagehands. And, of course, the children wanted to play with the puppets. Since they were glove puppets, we always let them. Anyway, the shyest kids you'd ever want to see were transformed once they were inside the box and pushed their hands up into the air.

Masks are like that. There is a book of masks called *The Alter Ego*. I don't know of a better title.

Masks were originally made for magical purposes. The hunter assumed the form of the beast he prepared to hunt in order to have magical power over it. Sometimes he took the forms of the high gods themselves in order to persuade them to do or not do, that is, to confer some benefit or call off the dogs.

One of the most effective masks of this type I've seen is from the Pacific Northwest and is in the American Museum of Natural History. It is made of painted wood, animated, and represents the sun and moon. There are four fish, equal in size and arranged in the form of a cross with their noses pointing outward, surrounding a quartered moon. They are hinged, and when they open, the sun is revealed. It is beautiful, made by a great craftsman. Devotees of the fat-cat cultural Alcatrazes that clutter our fruited plain would call it art. Aubrey Menen ties off that attitude with ease and grace in his "Prevalence of Witches" published in the *New York Times Magazine:*

"If by 'art' we mean something in which an artist expresses his personal self, then there is no such thing as primitive art. There are merely artifacts, which are used in the common run of ritual life—dances, consultations with the medicine man, anniversary celebrations, and the like. The taste and personality of the maker does not and must not enter into them. A tailor among us might take great care in cutting out a pair of evening trousers. But he would not use his scissors as a means of self expression, unless he meant to be contented with a very limited clientele. Thus, when nowadays I go to an exhibition of primitive art, I automatically look at it with the eyes of the Ashanti or Aztec or Ghanian. 'That mask,' I say, 'is a winner. It would scare the wits out of me deliciously if I saw it at midnight to the sound of drums'—which is what it was designed to do. I go no further in aesthetic appreciation."

The card in the display case containing the sun and moon mask has this message:

"These masks which represent supernatural beings were worn by dancers who performed in the winter ceremonies

211

One collection of Randy Echols' masks (this page) ranges from grotesqueries and animal heads to highly stylized and wire-haired half masks.

of the Bella Coola. The masks were carved during the ceremony and burned at its conclusion. The larger masks were carved out of beech and the smaller of alder. Each sculptor endeavored to make a striking effect with the result that even the Bella Coola with considerable knowledge could not always identify the supernatural being portrayed. The masks were painted; sometimes the painting identified the mask when the carving failed."

Well, maybe they're both right.

It would take a Robert Graves to make an educated try to find the thread of meaning that ties masks of prehistoric primitives to the ancient Greco/Roman drama and ceremonial masks, to medieval mummery, to the *commedia dell'arte*, to the Ball of Truman Capote.

As for Aubrey Menen's tailor having a very limited clientele if he tried to express himself in the cutting of the inexpressibles, a mask-maker for today's theatre has a very limited clientele. If a designer happens to be a little vague because of a preoccupation with how things are going at the scene shop or with a new baby, the mask-maker is apt to spread himself a bit. It's a long, long way from ritual—or maybe it isn't, if we pay attention.

As for Truman Capote's Ball, I have no idea what ritual was involved there. Maybe all his guests were delighted to wear masks because they simply were tired of looking at each other's celebrated faces. My wife made an angel-fish mask for Mrs. John Gunther, who had a very pointed and intelligent suggestion: "Please no sequins and/or feathers because everybody else will probably have them." They did, too. At least the guests had a basic advantage in the use of the masks while still maintaining their polite attitudes.

213

I'm *not* a Robert Graves, but I'd like to hazard one guess about the classic harlequin mask. One that's a dandy in a book entitled "Harlequin" is a dark leather half-mask with short, tightly-curled whiskers of what appears to be horse hair. There are very small holes for eyes and two bumps on the head. These bumps are too small for horns and one is not quite in the right place, but I think that they represent the horns beneath the skin trying to escape. I think the face may be a survival of the mask of the great god Pan himself, much changed by a rough passage through many centuries and two opulent religions as a devil, until he shows up in the *commedia dell arte.* But one thing is certain, taken by itself, it satisfies Aubrey Menen's criterion: it scares the hell out of me just to look at it on the printed page.

Aldous Huxley wrote in *The Doors of Perception:*

> "That humanity at large will ever be able to dispense with artificial paradises seems very unlikely. Most men and women lead lives at the worst so painful, at the least so monotonously poor and limited that the urge to escape, the longing to transcend themselves, if only for a few moments, is and always has been one of the principal appetites of the soul. Art and religion, carnivals and saturnalia, dancing and listening to oratory—all these have served in H. G. Wells' phrase as 'doors in the wall.'"

Masks have figured prominently in all of these except oratory. And even that has been referred to as a deep sound from the diaphragm masquerading as a message from the brain. So, what with the churches fighting to return to show business, maybe mask-making is looking up.

"In sculpture," said Jacob Epstein, "forms actually alter with the change of light." That seems simple enough. And certainly I have been exposed to this phenomenon often enough. I once saw a remarkable thing happen in the theatre perfectly illustrating this point. The play was ANGEL STREET, a rather plain little show about a man preparing to do his wife in and a detective who thwarts him.

214

The face of Vincent Price isn't really a mask within any meaning of the act, but it's pretty close. And Leo Carroll's is even closer. In a scene where the wife was sitting on a sofa facing directly front, Price took a slow walk around the sofa and ended behind her. A simple cross? An easy movement? I have never seen anything more menacing in my life. I questioned Lem Ayers, the designer, about it that very night.

"Oh," he said, "Feder lit the show and when Vincent took that walk he simply went through several planes of light, OK?"

"Yes," I said, "that seems right, and what about Carroll? When he pulled out the desk drawer and saw something that was supposed to astonish him, he actually looked astonished. I know Leo slightly; he's a monstrously witty fellow and I

admire his art, but I doubt if he's ever been astonished by anything at all."

"Oh that," said Lem, "Feder made a tiny spot, screwed it into the drawer and angled it up. Any more questions?"

"No," I said, "I think that'll hold me for now."

A puppet's face can be a mask, as we have seen, and it takes very little movement in any kind of light for it to change expression. My wife and I once built a whole show and played all parts, just to win an argument. The play was *The Dark Lady of the Sonnets* by Shaw. In Shaw one thing follows another with absolute logic and complete inevitability. The argument was that violence supposedly was the basis of all hand puppet shows since they lacked the flexibility of marionettes and so on. So we bet. I said we'd do an hour show and, with the exception of one sock in the jaw and one pratfall, without any violence—in fact without much action of any sort. We would present it to an audience without telling them the name of the play or the name of the playwright because his reputation would command an "em-

215

peror's-new-clothes" sort of attention even if *we* weren't any good.

We went into a summer hotel dining room, set up just as the victims were finishing dinner, and while they were still glassy-eyed from food and drink, our performance began without apology. It worked. It not only proved you don't need violence but you can read anything at all in a puppet's mask though the puppets may move hardly at all. I admit it was a little sneaky using Shaw. He sounds good no matter what—or almost no matter what.

The best example of this I know is the following: we had to build a figure of the Madonna for Boris Goldovsky's production of Massenet's opera *Le Jongleur de Notre Dame*. This was tricky since there was a scene where the audience had to see the monks painting the figure, another where she is carried in a procession, and another where she comes to life. The figure was made on a real girl, mask and all, and mounted on a rigid frame for the first two scenes, but the last scene the girl was inside. It was so well done that, when I watched it from the front, I said to myself, "she can't be inside it yet; there must be another scene break." But she was. And I was startled when she opened her arms to bless the sweating juggler and lowered her head just a fraction. Remember the opening of the sun and moon? And I, a hard bitten and crotchety relic, at least in matters theatrical, as you may have gathered, wept quiet tears of joy. Elliot Norton, who is, as you probably all know, a very hip character indeed, said when describing the scene in his review, "the Lady smiled." Now, if Mr. Norton had thought about it at all he would have known she did nothing of the kind since he had been looking at her for some time and her mask was obviously perfectly rigid. I find this very pleasant. Magic, you see. And light. You can't get a better notice than that.

Helmets can be masks, many are. The "Athena" helmet usually shown worn on the back with the mask in the position of a visor on a cap is one. Japanese medieval armor often had steel masks with stylized belligerent faces, sometimes with bushy horsehair moustaches. There are even a few European examples along this line. I should have remembered a Players' Club revival of *Troilus and Cressida* in the early thirties when Augustin as "a prologue armed" wore a helmet with a visor open and a spotlight straight down on the top of his head. You couldn't see his face at all. Wonderful.

I wonder if the *Macbird* helmet would qualify as a mask. Then it occurred to me that a mask doesn't have to cover the face at all, or even half the face. I completely forgot the most widely used type of mask that covers only the eyes—the classic domino. This is probably because it's not something to be made to order and can be bought in any candy store. Suddenly, I remembered that one of the greatest masks in history is no more than a pair of dark glasses worn by a young girl.

In William Seabrook's amazing book *The Magic Island* there is a photograph of a young girl as a "Papa Nebo" of the *cult des mortes:*

> "Before the altar of skulls, facing us, stood three human figures, grotesque, yet indescribably sinister. All three who stood there were women. The tall central figure, the former mild Classinia, now completely changed, wore a soft white muslin skirt, above it a man's longtailed black

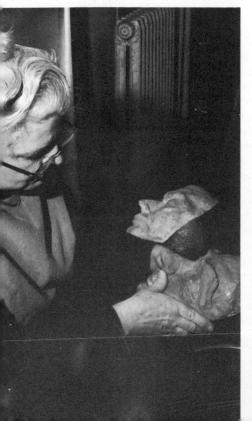

frock coat, and on her head a man's high silk hat; her eyes were hidden by dark, smoked goggles. Why it was that as simple a thing as smoked goggles seemed horrible, I cannot tell, unless because they made her face impersonal, inscrutable. Grotesquely in the corner of her mouth, as if stuck into the mouth of a wooden dummy, was an unlit cigar.

"Thus symbolically clothed, she was no longer a woman, but Papa Nebo, the male-female hermaphroditic oracle of the dead. The dark goggles meant that death was blind."

Her props are a scythe with a long handle held in her hand with a pick, a spade, and a skull at her feet. And as for the dark glasses, it's true they weren't as common in 1929 when this book was written as they are now. But I'm sure in Haiti they work just as well now as then.

I have no idea why it is that the Haitians seem not to have brought along masks of any kind from Africa. Actually I mean ideas for masks, because no one brings anything along when he is dragged from his home in chains. But then they brought along their ideas of music, dance, voodoo ceremonials, and there they are. Why not masks? Odd.

So masks don't have to cover the face. Eyes are enough. Again, looking at me every night at *Macbird* is a splendid set of masks that don't cover any part of the face; when the actors have finished their more or less conventional grease paint makeup, they cover their necks with clown white and draw a black line around their jawlines. Now, everyone has a mask. No one seems to remember whose idea this was— but it's all right, and I don't remember anything quite like it. An old Chinese proverb says: "There is darkness at the foot of the lighthouse."

218

But to go back to helmets for a moment. There is a yarn in Tennyson's *Idylls of the King* about a man who fights three brothers guarding three streams. The brothers have a terrifying reputation as knockabouts and they look terrifying too, because of their face armor, and especially their helmets. If I'm not mistaken they are called Morning, Noon and Night and they have to be fought at those times and on the same day. The third brother is death and mounted on a

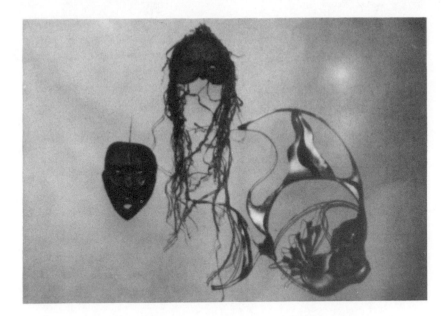

black horse. His helmet is in the form of a white death's head.

When our hero gets to this last one, he is, as you can imagine, bushed and upset at the sight of him. But courage is born of fear, so he hauls up his pauldrons and gives the apparition a mighty whack on the sconce with his two-handed sword. The helm is split in twain, falls to the ground —or as Tennyson would say—"Lo!" Who is sitting there on that crazy horse looking even more frightened than our hero? A kid, no less, the youngest of the three, who naturally surrenders at once. O.K.? I am told there is an ancient Irish legend that has much the same gimmick, except the scary one turns out to be a woman.

We made a roughed-in half-mask of the French actor Fernand Gravet for a play by Samuel Taylor where the leading man has a fake death mask made so that he can pretend that he has passed on to his reward. It's made of plastic wood right out of the can from a hardware store, because plaster would be too heavy and fragile. But it wasn't made from a life mask. My wife made it from caliper measurements of the actor's face and photographs. That's very tough, particularly since there was a scene in which the

219

actor had to hold it up to his own face. Years before, in Paris, someone had made a life mask of M. Gravet and in the doing, pulled his eyebrows out. He wasn't going through that again.

Last night after I had finished writing down these thoughts, I went to bed with my chiller which turned out to be *The Phantom of the Opera*. I hadn't read this since Lon Chaney made the silent movie, and this is what I found:

"None will ever be a true Parisian who has not learned to wear a mask of gaiety over his sorrows and one of sadness, boredom or indifference over his inward joy."

A pox on true Parisians. I hope their facial muscles sag to their knees for—

"I admire the fellow who is lively as a Kangaroo when everything is going right."

I don't remember who wrote that—but I love him.

In a world of professional specialization, the rise of the credit "Hair Designer" is a sign of our time. Ronald DeMann was one of the first to be credited in this way on Broadway; it was for his work on "The King and I" in 1951. The time was ripe for such a specilization and such continuing credits in the theatre. Late in the 1950s and during the 1960s, we witnessed the revival and popularization of that age symbolized by the whiplash, waving, wafting hair of women—the age of Art Nouveau; the 1960s also concluded with the international acceptance of a funky musical symbolizing the youth revolution with "Hair."

Ronald DeMann outlines the process of designing hair styles for a show, with particular reference to shows that require wigs. He discusses the process from initial consultations with the costume designer, through research—which is similar to the fascinating art-historical methodology described by costume designers in "The Theatre Crafts Book of Costume." Next, he goes on to describe working with wig houses, with actors at wig calls, and with budgets for wigs. Finally, he outlines wig maintenance for a Broadway show, the backstage readiness of a hair designer at every performance, and the cleaning methods that everyone should use. As a conclusion he adds a sobering comment on unions and apprenticeship in hair design.

In the 17 years he has been a hair de-

221

signer for the theatre, Ronald DeMann has *done an estimated 172 Broadway productions. Most of them were musicals, including, besides the ones he discusses, "The Boy Friend," "Sweet Charity," "Pajama Game," "Candide," "Can Can," and "Me and Juliet." Recently he has designed hair for "Two by Two," and "The Divorce of Judy and Jane."*

The following article was first published in "Theatre Crafts" in November/December, 1968.

More to Wigs than Hair

by Ronald DeMann

"Hair Designer" is a recent addition to the standard credits of a Broadway show. In the old days when a show called for wigs, the costume designer simply commissioned them from a wig maker, and the styling, the combing out, was trusted largely to the luck and ingenuity of the actors.

Since the costume designer is responsible for the overall look of a show, as hair designer I am essentially his lieutenant. Naturally, my first step in designing a show is to meet with him. At these sessions we discuss the general period we are working in, the costume designs that the hair styles will complement, and technical matters like the amount of time we'll have for costume changes.

Time was a primary concern of Costume Designer Irene Sharaff's and mine in *Hallelujah, Baby*. The show jumped decade by decade from 1900 to 1960. This meant that the star, Leslie Uggams, had to have seven different period hair styles. But the script often allowed her no more than a minute to make the complete change: costume, shoes and wig. In these situations we had the wigs ready for her in advance in quick-change rooms, located stage-left or stage-right. Sometimes she had even less than a minute to change, so we had to discard wigs and find simpler means of transforming her into a new period. Irene, for example, would then design a suitable cap.

While always working closely with the costume designer, I do my own independent research. I go to the theatre archives in the libraries, the style books and paintings of the period, and the costume histories. When I have culled through all the material and digested it, I create sketches and submit them to the costume designer for approval. Then the two of us decide on questions like color and texture. Or whether we need to take some theatrical license: vamp a wig—alter the length, raise the crown—so that it will be more becoming to a star without losing its period flavor.

I myself do not make wigs. Just as costume designers go to a costume house, I go to a wig house. There are many wig houses in New York that specialize in costume wigs; I pick the one that suits my needs and budget. But whichever house I choose can furnish me with two categories of wigs: custom-made and stock. All the wigs for the stars are generally in the first category. These are made from scratch out of the best hair you can buy—European hair—to the exact measurements of a star's head. Stock wigs are handmade, but since they are not custom-made, they usually require altering. For this reason we have hair calls. They actually come under the heading of costume calls, and since Equity permits only a limited number of costume calls, I'm lucky if I get the cast for two. Once a show goes out of town for try-outs, however, the cast is fair game: I and my staff wait around and pounce on them anytime they're not working.

A custom-made wig costs from $350 to $400; a stock wig, from $20 to $180. It's no wonder that I have to be constantly alert to ways of keeping the budget down. The normal wig budget for a show is about $3,000 or $3,500. But last fall I was hired to work on a show whose wig budget had been set at $8,000! And all that money went down the drain, for the show closed on the road.

*Ronald DeMann designed the hair styles
and wigs for "George M!" (above).*

Wig Maintenance

Once the wigs are ready and the show has opened, my job
is only half done. This does not mean I re-work and re-fix
the hair designs—I only do that when the costume designer
and I feel something should be altered to suit a cast replace-
ment. But my job is not just to design the hair styles; it is
to supervise their maintenance throughout the run of the
show.

Every show must have a hair dresser backstage every
night, both to set and style the wigs and to help the stars
with complicated costume changes. Since I often have several shows running simultaneously (at one point this winter
I had both the New York and Chicago companies of *Mame,
George M!* and *The Education of Hyman Kaplan*), I have a
stable of assistants who serve as backstage hair dressers. I

For the Broadway production of "Mame" with Jane Connell, Bea Arthur, and Angela Lansbury (above), Ronald DeMann designed hair and wigs, as he subsequently did for the film version with Rosalind Russell.

do the original cutting and styling of the wigs, then teach my assistants how to set and comb them. Usually I handle a show that is just starting myself, and from time to time check out the longer-running ones.

When I do a show, I guarantee that it will always be covered. If someone gets sick, I can generally substitute another assistant for him, or failing that, jump in myself. However, I do not hire out my hair dressers—or myself, for that matter—to shows I have not designed.

The actual maintenance of wigs entails nightly setting, styling and re-combing, and a weekly cleaning. To clean a wig you immerse it in Vapon, a cleaning fluid, and squeeze it until all the residue comes out. Just like working with human hair, except that because of the alcohol, a wig dries almost immediately. But you must be sure that the wig dries on a wig block. In fact, a wig should be placed on a wig block whenever it is not in use. Made to correspond with the size and shape of the head, the block preserves the form of the wig.

After a year or so of exposure to perspiration and constant cleaning a wig becomes fragile. But by repairing the foundation and adding more hair, you can make it as good as new. In *The Music Man* and *Funny Girl* the wigs lasted the entire run—three and a half years. Refurbishing, however, is not part of the hair dresser's maintenance responsibilities—the original wig maker does it, and it is not provided for in the weekly running expenses of the show.

There is one item under maintenance that I have not mentioned. It concerns men's hair in modern dress shows. Obviously, in a period play we take care of designing the men's hair as well as the women's. But in a modern dress show, unless the leading man wears a toupée, we have nothing to design for the men. Nonetheless we are often asked to maintain their hair—give them free hair cuts. Our contract does not require us to comply, but we do so willingly to maintain good public relations backstage.

Unions and Training

Since a number of my shows have been made into movies, people are always asking me why I haven't followed them out to Hollywood. The answer is simple: the movie hair designers have a practically closed union. Still, I have been able to do one and a half movies: 12 wigs for Rosalind Russell in *Auntie Mame* and Gwen Verdon's hair in *Damn Yankees*. When Miss Russell and Jack Warner got me into *Auntie Mame* an outsider hadn't worked for Hollywood in 30 years. And I never did learn how they got around the union problem.

The theatre, on the other hand, does not even have a hair designers' union. I negotiate separate contracts with every producer. Television does have a union, but it doesn't bar me from the medium. The television executives hire a stand-by hair dresser for me, so I am not putting anyone out of work and everyone's happy. But my schedule in the theatre does not leave much time for television, and I accept assignments only when one of the Broadway stars I work with appears on a program.

227

If you want to be a theatrical hair designer, the best way to go about it is to apprentice yourself to an established designer. To learn the business well you should allow three years of apprenticeship. And during this time you should be working right along with the designer; you should be learning on your own the hair styles and costumes of all the historical periods. There are only about four of us on Broadway who both design and maintain shows that have apprentices. I keep a list of talented hair dressers who have expressed interest in getting into the business, and I'm only too happy to use them when I can.

The manufacture of wigs, that is, realistic or naturalistic wigs made of hair, is beyond the purview of most hair designers and beyond the time and resources of most play producing groups. The process, as Bob Kelly describes it, stirs up a healthy respect for and considerate maintenance of well made wigs. It is a process that includes fitting the foundation, hair selection, treatment, and coloring; attachment or sewing, hair dressing, and styling. In the following interview, which was conducted by Sherwood Arthur, Bob Kelly also answers questions about the training of wig makers, the current sources of hair, the comparative problems that different media present to wig makers, the maintenance of wigs, and the process of ordering wigs from a rental house.

Bob Kelly demonstrates his open mind and ready interest in the overall field not only by the clear sighted activities of his firm—Bob Kelly Creations, which specializes in makeup as well as in wig making and rental—but also by his ready acknowledgement of the work of his colleagues.

228

Bob Kelly learned the craft of wigmaking as an apprentice to leading professionals of the Broadway stage and motion pictures. Among his clients are the television networks; the Shakespeare Festival in Stratford, Connecticut, the A.P.A. Repertory Company, the Lincoln Center Repertory Company, the New York City Opera Company, and the motion picture industry.

*Among the Broadway productions for which
he has supplied wigs are: "Dear World,"
"The Great White Hope," "Fiddler on the
Roof," "Golden Rainbow," "Plaza "Suite,"
and "Prisoner of Second Avenue."*

*Among the films for which he made wigs
are: "The Godfather," "Shaft," and "1776."*

*When the following article was first pub-
lished in "Theatre Crafts," September,
1969, Bob Kelly said that he would give new
attention to makeup and wigs for high
schools and the "Little Broadways across
the country." Since then he has lectured
widely on makeup in high schools as well as
preparing an impressive agenda for a series
of professional seminars on makeup to be
given in collaboration with Dick Smith.*

229

Twentieth Century Peruke Making

an interview with Bob Kelly

THEATRE CRAFTS: Mr. Kelly, will you tell us about the profession of making wigs for theatrical productions?

BOB KELLY: Wigmaking is one of the highest forms of art. There are only a handful of wigmakers in the U.S. who manufacture for theatre, and England is perhaps the only other country that manufactures wigs for theatrical, tv, and movie productions.

TC: Will you tell us the procedure of making wigs from raw hair to finished products, once you are assigned to a Broadway show?

BK: The director, the costume designer, and I meet to look at the sketches and to decide upon which colors and shapes we want for the wig for a particular actor or actress. After fitting the actor or actress with a foundation, which is like a cap over the head, I select a wooden block and mark the actor's measurements on it. I select the colors that the costume designer and I have agreed upon. Then we are ready to start construction. First we boil the hair—sometimes we bleach it, but always we dye it. Then we draw the hair for different lengths. In one piece there may be as many as ten

231

Eighteenth Century wigs rely on traditional documents such as the engraved advertisement by William Hogarth, dated October 15, 1761, on page 230. Included there are five orders of periwigs as they were worn at the Coronation of George III.

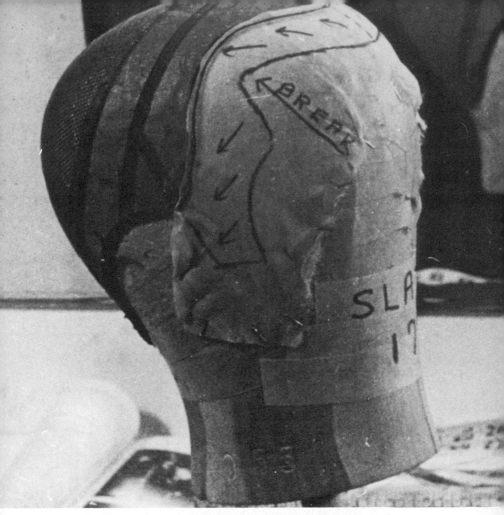

In the process of wig making, a foundation is constructed and mounted on a head form (above). The completed foundation is the exact size of the actor's head and the form is accompanied with hair color samples before it goes into production for hair blending, ventilating, and styling.

or twelve different lengths of hair, from six to twenty inches. We take many different colors and blend them together in order to obtain the particular hair color we want. Then the hair is ready for the ventilator—the technician (usually a girl) who places it, strand by strand into the wig foundation with a crochet hook. But first I draw the pattern on the foundation indicating with arrows which directions the hair is to be put. This ventilation process takes approximately two and one-half to three days.

Hair is placed, strand by strand, into the foundation with a crochet hook (above); this operation is called "ventilating."; A wig for "1776" on a head form before final styling (above).

TC: What is the next step?

BK: Now the wig is ready for the hair-dressing department. Mind you, the wig is still on the wooden block. The hairdresser, having studied the original sketch for the desired style, shapes the wig and fashions and dresses it to look just like the sketch. Then we take the "creation" to the production company, where the actor or actress tries it on for the director's approval. He may not like the wig—or the style or the color—at this point we get the good or the bad news, and we follow the director's orders.

TC: How does one train for the wig profession?

233

BK: Usually those who enter this profession have been hairdressers first. In my company we have approximately thirty employees, many of whom have come to this country from Europe and the Caribbean. These people have the tradition of fine craftsmanship necessary for wigmaking. I was taught this business by wigmaker Ira Senz, who is one of the foremost wigmakers in the industry, and I have been able to share my knowledge and experience with my employees—who in turn have trained our new workers as they are employed. There are no schools in the field of theatrical wigmaking. One learns by experiment and from being shown by experienced craftsmen.

TC: Then it is impossible to learn wigmaking in high schools and colleges today?

BK: I think it would be difficult ,because it would take someone with a great deal of technical knowledge and experience to teach wigmaking in school. Also, institutions might not offer sufficient opportunities for one to learn the creation of a variety of wig types.

TC: What kind of hair is used for making wigs?

BK: First, it requires a tremendous stock of raw hair. We sometimes use the hair from yaks, a long haired ox that is found in Tibet and Central Asia, but most of the time we use human hair from India, Philippines, Indonesia, Italy, and Germany. We used to buy a lot of Korean hair, until the government of Korea placed an embargo on it. Our own government has restrictions on hair imported from European countries, because it is trying to prevent an infiltration of hair from communist countries. Wig manufacturers have to prove to our government where they have purchased hair with a Certificate of Origin. In addition, when Italian hair is purchased, a manufacturer must be able to prove the quantity with the bill of sale. Undoubtedly some hair is shipped illegally.

TC: What do you consider the best hair for wigmaking?

234

BK: If the design is to be of best quality, European hair is preferable because of its texture and softness. Hair that comes from countries where there is a lot of poverty is suitable only for certain "less quality" wigs. Today, unfortunately, there is a shortage of hair. The older generations are dying off and the younger generation that is still willing to have haircuts wears shorter hair styles.

TC: Which medium presents the most difficult problems in designing wigs?

BK: Motion pictures. When there is a close-up in cameras, it is usually extreme; if the wig is not natural looking, an actor can appear ridiculous. Also, wigs must be natural looking for tv shows, whereas heavier materials can sometimes be used for stage productions, since the wigs are seen from a distance. One movie that was challenging was "No Way To Treat A Lady," for which I designed all the wigs for Lee Remick and Rod Steiger. Rod Steiger had many dis-

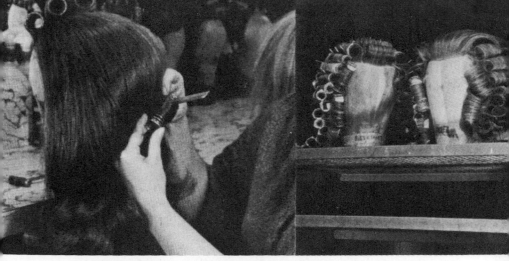

*Wigs are placed in drying ovens (right), which are
humidity controlled to ensure that each wig will both
look right and also hold its shape under different
temperature conditions on and off stage.*

guises in this movie, including his impersonation of a
woman, and each character had to look authentic and natural.

TC: What was the most difficult assignment you have had?

BK: One wig might be more time consuming than another—
but difficult, no! Perhaps my most time-consuming show was
"Rashomon," which was performed many years ago on tv.
The period of time in Japanese history was Samurai, when
feudal Japan had knights who wore their hair "styled up"
beginning at the nape of the neck. The research came basically from the costume designer who gave me the sketches
he wanted, but the wigs became time consuming because we
had to "lace" them in back to make them look like the hair
met the nape without a harsh hair line. For those, we used
Indian hair because it was naturally black.

TC: What do you mean when you say to "lace" them?

BK: To lace is to put each individual hair into a very fine
mesh, so that the hair looks like it is growing out of the
head. The process is usually installed on the front of the wig
only, to cover the front hair line in order to make it look
real; normally, the rest of the wig can be made with heavier
materials in which three or four strands can be put into
each hole.

TC: Do you manufacture men's hairpieces?

BK: Yes, and hair for mustaches, beards, sideburns—and chest hair as well. We made chest hair for Martin Balsam in "You Know I Can't Hear You When The Water Is Runing" and for Dustin Hoffman for "Jimmy Shine," in which he would rip off his chest piece for a gag.

TC: What are the problems of period wigs?

BK: Unlike a modern wig for which one may need only to comb bangs on a bouffant short piece, the design of a wig for George Washington's day requires more difficult styling and combing. This design also has various lengths of hair and a different type of foundation. For a Marie Antionette wig, the hair is piled high upon the head. A wire cage, approximately twelve inches high, must be built to go on top of the foundation; hair is sewn over the wire cape to give it the proper height. If we are to design a Moliere wig, we must make extremely long flaps which go below the breast; two more flaps are needed to go down each arm and another flap to go down the back. On these flaps we stitch additional short hair.

TC: How are the wigs maintained while they are in use in a play?

BK: When a Broadway show doesn't have a hair stylist who maintains wigs, the show is in trouble, because most actors and actresses don't know how to care for them. There is a definite art to putting a wig on a head and to combing it. Although it doesn't need to be rolled or styled before each performance, it should be combed properly, before each use. A wig also should be cleaned properly, particularly if it has a lace front which requires the use of a spirit gum glue. Right now I am maintaining the wigs for "Plaza Suite": every Monday the wigs are sent to me for re-styling, and during the week the show's stylist keeps the wigs combed and cleaned of glue.

TC: Are there catalogues available from which an actor can order wigs?

BK: Yes, but the best thing for an actor to do is to refer to Richard Corson's book "Fashions In Hair" which contains 500 pages covering every style in history. If this book is not available to the actor, he can cut a sketch out of a magazine or have a photostat made from a reference source in his local library to send to the wig designer. If he orders a wig from us, he must send the head measurements, the desired colors, and either a picture or the page number from Corson's book. We have so many wigs in our stock—approximately eight thousand—that we could probably supply his wig without creating a new one; if not, then we would create a new one.

TC: When a wig is rented from you, is it possible for you to restyle it for later use?

BK: Yes, when the wig is returned to us we clean it well and then give it a new style.

TC: Are there any problems in your profession?

BK: Yes. One problem is that most of the wigmakers for theatre are old fashioned craftsmen who may be used to materials such as cotton that were used in the first part of this century. These can end up looking ridiculous. Another unfortunate situation in my profession is that many wigs are made of dynel; these wigs are very difficult to style and easily lose their shapes. There is no substitute for hair! Another misfortune is the poor quality of wigs available for use by colleges, high schools, and community theatres. I personally hope to concentrate on these areas, and to produce wigs of higher quality at more reasonable prices for their use.

TC: When you send a wig for rental, do you include instructions for use and care?

BK: Yes, we always include instructions. We also encourage our clients to visit our shop when possible, so that we can teach wearers how to handle the wigs. We take them through the shop and try to enlighten them on the procedures used in styling and handling. When possible, I will invite a famous hair stylist, such as Ernest Adler, to give demonstrations to the group on how to put on hair pieces and how to make fast changes in plays. We all benefit from these demonstrations. There is always something new to be learned to improve my trade. Those of us in this profession love it and hope everyone in theatre will share our enthusiasm. Perhaps from increased interest we will draw more artists so there will be no doubt that there is a wigmaker left in the Twentieth Century.

238